# DEFUSING
# DISRUPTIVE
# BEHAVIOR
## IN THE CLASSROOM

*To my mother, Joan, my late father, Clem, and late parents-in-law, Betty and Don:*
*Who fared with less so we could have more.*

# DEFUSING
# DISRUPTIVE
# BEHAVIOR
## IN THE CLASSROOM

# GEOFF COLVIN
Foreword by Robert H. Horner

**CORWIN**
A SAGE Company

*For information:*

Corwin
A SAGE Company
2455 Teller Road
Thousand Oaks, California 91320
(800) 233-9936
Fax: (800) 417-2466
www.corwin.com

SAGE India Pvt. Ltd.
B 1/I 1 Mohan Cooperative
  Industrial Area
Mathura Road, New Delhi 110 044
India

SAGE Ltd.
1 Oliver's Yard
55 City Road
London EC1Y 1SP
United Kingdom

SAGE Asia-Pacific Pte. Ltd.
33 Pekin Street #02-01
Far East Square
Singapore 048763

Printed in the United States of America

*Library of Congress Cataloging-in-Publication Data*

Colvin, Geoffrey, 1941-
Defusing disruptive behavior in the classroom / Geoff Colvin; foreword by Robert H. Horner.
      p. cm.
Includes bibliographical references and index.
ISBN 978-1-4129-8056-2 (pbk.)
   1. Classroom management. 2. Problem children—Behavior modification. I. Title.

LB3013.C558 2010
371.102'4—dc22                                      2010012051

This book is printed on acid-free paper.

10   11   12   13   14   10   9   8   7   6   5   4   3   2   1

| | |
|---|---|
| *Acquisitions Editor:* | Jessica Allan |
| *Associate Editor:* | Joanna Coelho |
| *Editorial Assistant:* | Allison Scott |
| *Production Editor:* | Eric Garner |
| *Copy Editor:* | Adam Dunham |
| *Typesetter:* | C&M Digitals (P) Ltd. |
| *Proofreader:* | Joyce Li |
| *Indexer:* | Sheila Bodell |
| *Cover Designer:* | Scott Van Atta |

# *Contents*

# *Foreword*

*Robert H. Horner*

**B**ehaviors such as aggression, defiance, insubordination, and disruption continue to be the most common reasons why children are excluded from schools. In this book Geoff Colvin focuses on the critical interactions between students and teachers that can transform escalating problems into effective resolutions. The themes throughout this book are clear. Children respond more effectively to classrooms that are predictable, consistent, positive, and safe. Making both schoolwide and classroom expectations clear from the beginning is an essential start. But defining, teaching, and recognizing appropriate behavior will not prevent all behavior problems. Situations will still occur where the verbal or physical behavior of a student crosses the line.

This book assumes that basic classroom and schoolwide management practices are in place, and focuses the reader on interactions at the moment of conflict. I have read each of Dr. Colvin's books and see the same humor, wisdom, and practical value in this book that have been the hallmarks of his earlier work. Colvin draws from his experience in classroom and administrative roles. He brings a voice to this complex problem that is at once accessible, scientifically valid, and practical. This is a book written for teachers and I expect it to be of real value to them. It is organized to provide very specific, usable recommendations. The checklists and vignettes give teachers a framework for both assessing current practice and identifying steps to make their classroom more effective.

The major contribution of this text is the organization of basic behavioral concepts within a practical framework that informs daily experience. Seven "principles" for understanding problem behavior are introduced in the opening chapter, and these principles are used to frame specific solutions for addressing off-task behavior, rule infraction, disrespect, agitation, and noncompliance. While a wealth of content is braided into the messages provided in each chapter, two core messages provide the overarching theme that effective classroom management is possible.

The first message lies in Geoff Colvin's emphasis on the active relationship between students and teachers. Students seldom behave badly in a vacuum. Through his use of vignettes and stories, Colvin shows how most problem behaviors emerge through the give and take of normal daily classroom activity. It is useful to follow the multiple steps that allow a comparatively innocuous problem to escalate into a major behavioral violation. Student behavior is described in clear and memorable precision, but the book keeps bringing us back to the message that the major behavioral violation emerged through several teacher–student interchanges. We see how the student behavior is guided in response to teacher behavior, and of equal importance, we see how teacher behavior is prompted and shaped by student behavior. Problem behavior in the classroom typically is a behavioral conversation, not an independent act in isolation. The message Geoff Colvin brings from his elegant description of the "interaction pathway" is that if you understand your role in the interaction you can change the trajectory of the path. There will be many teacher–student conversations that start off on a negative note, but how the path is managed can affect if that student remains in class as an active learner, or is dismissed. This book is about how to manage the interaction so both the student and the teacher succeed. Understanding how the give and take of an interaction can become an escalating chain leading to dangerous behavior is useful for understanding how to preempt the negative trajectory. More than anything, Geoff Colvin helps us see how the context we create can make a difference, and how a behavior problem affects all involved.

The second major message threaded through the book is the powerful impact of consequences. Not just the positive and negative consequences we intend to deliver, but the impact of consequences as students experience them. Multiple vignettes, for example, describe the powerful role of teacher attention (even negative teacher attention) as a controlling consequence. Attend to behaviors you want and they are likely to increase. Attend to behaviors you do NOT want and they also are likely to increase. A great asset in schools is that teacher attention is rewarding for students. Too often we are inadvertently drawn into situations where we are attending to behaviors we do not want: "Jason, please sit down" . . ."Marla, you are not doing what I asked." A frustrating irony lies in the consistent message that attending to problem behavior is very likely to encourage problem behavior. The enlightening resolution lies in Colvin's simple, effective recommendations for how to use teacher attention constructively, and avoid inadvertent reward of problem behaviors. He encourages us to emphasize the positive, correct behavioral errors without drawing class attention or extensive teacher attention to the errors, and to repeatedly self-assess how teacher behavior can be changed to produce the improvements we desire in students.

This is a book about making classrooms more effective. It is a book for experienced teachers who already use the basic prevention and reward practices that are part of schoolwide and classroom behavior management. In this text Geoff Colvin takes us through that next level of more difficult interactions. He focuses on the teacher behaviors that will help students succeed. He encourages the self-reflection about how teachers can both prevent problems from occurring, and prevent those problems that do occur from escalating into major behavioral infractions. He holds students responsible for their behavior, but also gives teachers guidance for how we can create schools where more students succeed. Teachers will benefit from the precision, clarity, and utility of his recommendations. Students will benefit from classrooms that are more predictable, consistent, positive, and safe.

# *Acknowledgments*

I wish to especially acknowledge two longtime colleagues of mine for their helpful exchanges and collaboration over many years and particularly for their significant input to core concepts in this book.

First is Rob Horner, for his earlier pioneer work on behavioral chains in vocational training for adults with disabilities, published in the then-famous *Red Book*. Since that time, Rob has helped me apply this concept to other behaviors, especially problem behavior. It is through this communication with Rob that I have extended the concept of behavioral chains to interaction pathways, a cornerstone of this book.

Second, I wish to acknowledge the ongoing communications I have had with George Sugai on the challenge of helping teachers to modify or abandon behavioral practices that are ineffective and adopt strategies that have more likelihood of success. George has helped me to focus on initial responses from teachers. In particular, he has highlighted the need to assist teachers in becoming more fluent with these more-productive initial responses—another cornerstone of this book.

Also, I wish to thank Tina Wells for her insightful editing comments and constructive feedback on the layout and flow of the book. Tina is just amazing in how she can attend to minute details and, at the same time, quickly comprehend big ideas and make significant contributions at that level.

Finally, I wish to thank all of the teachers in the field who on a daily basis are subjected to a huge number of challenges, pressures, and expectations from so many sources. But, when it comes down to it, where would we be without our teachers? I offer them my thanks and appreciation.

Additionally, Corwin would like to thank the following peer reviewers for their editorial insight and guidance:

Dawne Dragonetti
Special Education Teacher, Instructional Coach
Nashoba Regional School District
Stow, MA

Mari Gates
Fifth-Grade Inclusion Teacher
Henry B. Burkland Intermediate School
Middleboro, MA

Robin Kuketz
Fifth-Grade Inclusion Teacher
Henry B. Burkland School
Middleboro, MA

# *About the Author*

 **Geoff Colvin** draws on his experience as a classroom teacher, both in special and general education, school administrator, educational consultant, and research associate at the University of Oregon.

He is a nationally recognized educational consultant who has assisted personnel in more than 200 school districts and agencies, nationally and internationally, on the subject of managing problem behavior, teaching challenging students, and school safety planning.

He has authored and coauthored more than 80 publications, including the very popular book *Managing the Cycle of Acting-Out Behavior in the Classroom* and the 2000 Telly Award–winning video program "Defusing Anger and Aggression." His recent book *7 Steps for Developing a Proactive Schoolwide Discipline Plan* has achieved bestseller status with Corwin.

As an administrator, he directed a juvenile detention school for five years and was the principal of a countywide school for youth with serious emotional disturbances for five years. He served as the supervisor of special programs with Bethel School District, Eugene, Oregon, for several years, where he still serves as a consultant.

Dr. Colvin has a very special skill in being able to translate theory into practice. He is able to present clear explanations and analyses of learning and behavior and at the same time offer concrete examples with hands-on illustrations. He has a very strong insightful understanding of the relationship between quality instruction and behavior management. His extensive knowledge and experience base, lively speaking style, and keen sense of humor have made him a highly sought-after speaker at national and international conferences.

In March, 2010, he became the first recipient of the Lifetime Achievement Award for the Northwest Positive Behavior Interventions and Supports (PBIS). Presently, he serves as a national educational and behavioral consultant.

# Introduction

*Among the top reasons why teachers are deemed unsuccessful or leave the profession is their inability to effectively manage student behavior, experts say.*

—Seema Mehta, "Controlling a Classroom Isn't as Easy as ABC,"
*Los Angeles Times*, December 14, 2009

One of the biggest challenges facing classroom teachers today is the ongoing need to address problem behavior. In addition to this challenge, teachers are subjected to many other pressures on a daily basis, such as the need to increase achievement scores, effectively teach to students with diverse needs, and increase capacity to serve all students, often with decreasing funds and support. One fact remains clear: These goals cannot be achieved unless teachers are equipped with sound classroom-management techniques designed to establish the kind of classroom environment necessary to support quality instruction and student learning.

Many successful approaches have been identified in published literature and best practices in schools for addressing problem behavior and for establishing desirable classroom behavior. These approaches include the systematic application of proactive systems and strategies for preventing problem behavior and teaching desirable behavior. In addition, there are many effective correction strategies for following up on occurrences of problem behavior aimed at reducing future occurrences of these behaviors and increasing rates of desirable behavior. These strategies target problem behavior *before* it has a chance to occur and *after* it has occurred, both of which are absolutely necessary for classroom management.

However, there is another window for managing problem behavior, and that is strategies for responding to behavior *immediately following its occurrence*. Many teachers have experienced the situation where they attempted to correct a problem behavior and ended up with a worse one—which means that the procedure used escalated the problem rather than corrected it. For example, a student throws some paper on the floor while

1

the teacher is explaining something. The teacher stops the explanation and tells the student that it is not acceptable to disrupt the class and directs the student to pick up the paper. The student mumbles a disrespectful comment, further discussion ensues resulting in the student being sent to the time-out area for disrespect. In this vignette, the student begins by throwing paper on the floor and ends with displaying disrespectful behavior and is removed to time-out with loss of instruction time for the teacher and the rest of the class. The way the teacher responded to the initial problem behavior, throwing paper on the floor, more than likely escalated the student to display disrespect, resulting in removal and loss of instruction time. Suppose the teacher, instead of responding to the initial behavior of the student, maintained the explanation, directed the class to the class activity, then approached the student privately and asked the student to retrieve the paper and put it where it needed to be. In this vignette, the student would be less likely to disrupt the class, exhibit disrespectful behavior, and be removed from the class to the time-out area.

The purpose of this book is to present strategies for responding to problem behavior in a way that is more likely both to defuse the situation by avoiding escalation and to correct the problem. The primary focus is to examine the initial response to the different kinds of common behaviors teachers face in classrooms. The rationale for this book is that this initial response, by and large, determines what the student or students may do next. In this sense, it is this initial response and subsequent *interactions* that determine the direction of the student behavior.

*Defusing Problem Behavior in the Classroom* is primarily designed for teachers as they are the front line for addressing problem behavior in schools, especially in classrooms, where students spend most of their time at school. The information should also be useful to specialists and behavior-support teams who have the responsibility of assisting teachers with managing challenging and persistent behavioral issues. Finally, these procedures for managing interactions have relevance for administrators who are charged with following up directly student office referrals and other serious behavior.

There are six chapters in this book. Chapter 1, Seven Key Behavioral Principles, opens with an examination of the relationship between teacher-student interactions, when problem behavior is being addressed, and subsequent student behavior. Guidelines based on sound behavioral research and best practices are presented for managing these interactions to ensure that the student's behavior is not escalated and that appropriate behavior is obtained. These behavioral principles are then applied in detail in the following chapters to defuse the most common problem behaviors teachers face in K–12 classrooms: Chapter 2, Defusing Off-Task Behavior; Chapter 3, Defusing Rule Infractions; Chapter 4, Defusing Disrespectful Behavior; Chapter 5, Defusing Agitation; and Chapter 6, Defusing Noncompliance and Limit Testing. Five topics are addressed in each chapter: (1) description of the problem behavior;

(2) prerequisite conditions; (3) illustration, Grades K–12; (4) defusion steps for addressing the problem behavior; and (5) application. In Chapter 2, three illustrations are presented for student groupings (kindergarten and elementary, secondary, and specialist classes) to demonstrate the range of application for the defusing strategies. In Chapters 3 through 6, one example per chapter is selected to sample the student groupings. A practice example is also provided at the end of these chapters, followed by a response key in the Appendices at the end of the book.

In Closing Remarks, the main ideas of the book are summarized. Reproducible forms, checklists, and response keys to the practice problems are presented in the Appendices.

# 1

# *Seven Key Behavioral Principles*

The focus in this book is defusing strategies for teachers to use at the very *onset* of problem behavior. It may be that the teacher makes good use of proactive strategies to both prevent problem behavior and to establish expected behavior and may have best-practice procedures in place for following up with problem behavior. However, problem behavior will still occur because of factors that cannot be directly controlled in the classroom. For example, the students may engage in counterproductive behaviors outside of school time, which reinforce problem behavior. These behaviors may then spill over to the classroom. How the teacher responds to the occurrence of problem behavior is the theme of this book. However, before specific strategies are described for directly responding to these common problem behaviors (Chapters 2–7), seven key behavioral principles that underlie the strategies need to be clearly understood. These seven principles are described in this chapter: (1) goals of correction procedures; (2) the role of teacher attention in correction procedures; (3) the nature of behavioral intensity, escalation, and defusion; (4) the nature of behavioral chains; (5) the role of behavioral extinction and extinction bursts; (6) the power of personal reactions; and (7) establishing fluent responses.

# KEY PRINCIPLE ONE: GOALS OF CORRECTION PROCEDURES

When students display problem behavior in the classroom, teachers have an initial goal of interrupting the problem behavior and directing the students to engage in appropriate behavior. For example, if the teacher is explaining something to the class, and two students are talking to each other, the teacher may ask them to stop talking and listen to the explanations. Ideally, the students will cease talking to each other and listen to the teacher. However, while this result is necessary, it may not be sufficient. Regarding the same example, suppose the students follow the teacher's prompt to cease talking and listen, but they resume talking a few minutes later or begin talking to each the following day when the teacher is again explaining something. The students cooperated initially but resumed the same problem behavior later. The problem behavior was not corrected. An effective correction procedure must have the goal of not only interrupting the problem behavior and redirecting the students to the expected behavior but also ensure appropriate behavior in future situations.

Teachers utilize these same two steps for correcting academic errors. When students make errors in a subject, the teacher informs them that an error has been made, assists them to correct the error, and expects the students to make correct responses to similar tasks in the future. If errors persist, the teacher typically adjusts the correction procedures to ensure future correct responses.

The first goal for correcting problem behavior is to interrupt the problem behavior and engage the students in the expected behavior. The second goal is to ensure the students exhibit the expected behavior in future occurrences of similar situations.

There is a third goal in addressing problem behavior, which is critical in this book, and that is to avoid escalation or accelerating the problem behavior. Suppose, for example, in the earlier illustration with the two students talking while the teacher was explaining something to the class, the teacher stopped talking very suddenly, glared at the two students, and told them that they were very rude for disrupting the class. One of the students muttered something to the other student who laughed. The teacher then walked to the two students, demanding to know what was said. Meanwhile, the whole class is watching this interaction. One of the students said nothing was said, and the other grinned. Both students were then sent to the office for disrespect and disrupting the class. Clearly, the situation *escalated,* beginning with two students talking and ending with each of them removed from class for additional behaviors of disrespect and disruption. In later chapters, detailed information will be described for not only addressing the initial problem behavior effectively but also decreasing the likelihood of escalating the situation. The third goal in correcting problem behavior is to avoid escalation.

The three main goals in correcting problem behavior are summarized in Box 1.1.

---

**BOX 1.1**
**Three Main Goals in Correcting Problem Behavior**

1. Interrupt the problem behavior, and engage the student or students in the expected behavior.

2. Ensure the student or students exhibit the expected behavior in future occurrences of similar situations.

3. Avoid escalating the situation to more serious behavior.

---

## KEY PRINCIPLE TWO: THE ROLE OF TEACHER ATTENTION IN CORRECTION PROCEDURES

Teacher attention plays a powerful role in affecting the whole gamut of student behavior from establishing expected behavior (Darch & Kame'enui, 2004; Sprick, Garrison, & Howard, 1998), reducing problem behavior (Algozzine & Kay, 2001), maintaining behavior (Carr & Shabani, 2005), and escalating problem behavior (Colvin, 2004; Sprick & Garrison, 2008). Of particular interest in this book is the role teacher attention plays in correcting problem behavior and in escalating or defusing these behaviors.

Several years ago Becker (1986) described an insightful, almost comical, study that clearly illustrated how a teacher was simultaneously correcting a problem behavior and reinforcing the same problem behavior simply as a function of teacher attention. Observers recorded the number of times a first-grade teacher told someone in the class to sit down and the number of students who were not sitting down in a 10-second interval for 20 minutes over a period of six days for each phase of the study. There were five phases in the study.

**Phase 1—Baseline:** In a 10-second interval, the average number times the teacher told someone to sit down was approximately once, and the average number of students standing up was approximately three.

**Note:** It is important to realize that the students followed the direction to sit down in all instances in this study.

**Phase 2—First Intervention:** The teacher was asked to catch more students not sitting down and give them the direction to sit down. The average number of students not sitting down increased to 4.3 (from 3), and the number of teacher directions to sit down averaged three per interval (from 1).

**Phase 3—Reversal:** The teacher was asked to resume the initial practice of responding to some of the students not sitting down. In this phase, the number of students not sitting down decreased to the baseline average of about three per interval and the number of directions from the teacher reduced to about one per interval.

**Phase 4—Second Reversal:** The teacher was then asked to increase the number of directions to sit down to all students who were standing up. The results showed a corresponding increase in the number of students standing up to averaging 4.5 per interval and the teacher directions to sit down increasing to about four per interval.

**Final Phase—Second Intervention:** The teacher was asked to ignore the students not sitting down and to praise the students who were sitting down and working. In this phase, the number of students not sitting down was recorded at two, the lowest of any phase.

The results from this study were compelling and obvious:

1. The more times the teacher told the students to sit down, the more students stood up.

2. The teacher's direction to "sit down" became the cue for other students, already seated, to stand up—the very behavior the teacher was trying to stop.

3. The students who were told to sit down cooperated and sat down on each occasion.

4. The least number of students standing up occurred when the teacher ignored the ones standing and praised those who were seated and working (Becker, 1986).

The overall conclusion from this study was that the behavior the teacher directly attended to was increased. Or, the most effective strategy for obtaining the expected behavior of sitting down was to directly acknowledge those students who were seated and working and ignore the students who were not seated. Moreover, the study highlighted the common *teacher-attention trap* of addressing a problem behavior, obtaining cooperation, and yet maintaining the problem behavior.

The author has frequently used an activity in presentations to educators to obtain a similar result explaining the role of teacher attention in maintaining problem behavior. Participants are asked to wave their hands if they agree to any of the following three statements:

1. All students, regardless of age, need some level of teacher attention. Participant response: *All wave their hands.*

2. Good behavior, expected behavior, is *guaranteed* to obtain teacher attention (emphasis on the word *guaranteed*). Participant responses: *No hands wave.*

3. Bad behavior, serious problem behavior, is *guaranteed* to obtain teacher attention. Participant response: *All participants wave their hands.*

The conclusion drawn from this activity is that the surest way to obtain teacher attention is to misbehave.

Some fundamental principles related to the role of teacher attention in correcting problem behavior are summarized in Box 1.2.

---

**BOX 1.2**
**Role of Teacher Attention in Correcting Problem Behavior**

1. All students need teacher attention to some extent.

2. Problem behavior is a sure way of obtaining teacher attention.

3. When teachers respond directly to students displaying problem behavior, they are providing attention to these students who may not otherwise be receiving teacher attention.

4. Even though students may comply with a direction, they may exhibit the same problem at a later time, indicating that the behavior has been reinforced by the teacher's correction procedure.

5. Other students who are cooperating may begin to display the problem behavior in order to receive teacher attention.

6. Teacher attention, if properly directed, can be used to reinforce expected behavior and reduce problem behavior.

---

## KEY PRINCIPLE THREE: THE NATURE OF BEHAVIORAL INTENSITY, ESCALATION, AND DEFUSION

It was noted earlier that when teachers address problem behavior, one of the goals is to avoid escalation or accelerating the behavior to more serious concerns. It is very important to have a solid working understanding to these related terms: behavioral intensity, escalation, and defusion.

*Behavioral intensity* is a measure of the seriousness of the behavior. For example, the problem behavior of talking out in class is less serious or less intense than the behavior of throwing a chair across the room. Behavioral intensity is usually measured by the impact of the behavior in relation to a number of variables, such as classroom disruption, safety for the individual and others, and personal and social needs of the students. Each of these factors has a number of levels or degrees of intensity. For example, a student throwing a paper airplane could be considered dangerous if it hit someone in the eye. However, a student throwing a chair is a more serious or more intense behavior because, compared to throwing a paper airplane, there is more likelihood of someone being hurt. Similarly, when a single student calls another student a nasty name on one occasion, there is a chance that the recipient of the abuse may be offended. However, if several students, singly or in a group, call an individual student a name on several occasions, there is much more chance the recipient will be offended and bothered by the sustained verbal attacks. The sustained attacks are considered to have higher intensity compared to the single-instance attack.

*Behavior escalation* is the process when a student, or group of students, exhibits a behavior that begins with low intensity and moves to higher intensities as a result of certain conditions. For example, two students may be arguing over whose turn it is to use the computer. Neither student gives way, so they begin to call each other names, pushing, and punching before the teacher is able to get to them. The successive student behaviors of arguing, name calling, pushing, and punching show increasing intensity, that is, the behaviors have escalated. Similarly, a student has his head down on his desk in class and the teacher asks him to begin work. He says he is finished, and the teacher checks and finds the student has barely started. The teacher tells him he has much more to do and needs to get on with it. The student says he is not interested and does not plan to work any more. The teacher tells him that if he needs help to ask for it, otherwise he can do the work now, or he will have to do it during the break. The student utters an expletive and shouts, "No way." The teacher tells him he needs to go to the time-out area. In this vignette, the successive behaviors of the student (off-task with head down on the desk, false claim that the work has been completed, refusal to start work, and uttering expletives) show increasing intensity, namely, the behavior has escalated.

*Behavioral defusion* is an antonym for behavioral escalation. Defusion is the process when a student's behavior shows successive decreases in intensity. For example, a student may be shouting out angry responses in class. The teacher intervenes, then the student begins to mumble to herself and a short time later sits with arms folded, staring at the floor. The teacher intervenes again, and the student reluctantly picks up her pen and begins to write. The sequence of behaviors displayed by the student is shouting in class, mumbling to herself, sitting staring at the floor and not working, and slowly beginning to work. These successive behaviors show a reduction in intensity indicating that the situation has been defused.

This concept of defusion is central to the strategies used in addressing problem behavior and appears in the title of this book and in chapter headings. It is critical for teachers to understand that the student's behavior is *heading in the right direction* and that it may take several steps before the student is clearly on task appropriately. One teacher, in the example above, may conclude that the student has stopped shouting but is now sitting there refusing to work, and the teacher may mistakenly respond directly to the so-called noncompliance and thereby escalate the student's behavior. Another teacher, in the same situation, may conclude the student is now heading in the right direction, and the teacher continues to calmly and positively redirect the student. This teacher ends up with the student on task, whereas the other teacher ends up with an escalated situation.

The key principles related to behavioral intensity, escalation, and defusion are summarized in Box 1.3.

---

### BOX 1.3
### Key Points for Behavioral Intensity, Escalation, and Defusion

1. *Behavioral intensity* is a measure of the seriousness of a behavior based on its impact related to classroom disruption, safety, and personal and social factors.

2. *Behavioral escalation* is the process where a student engages in a series of behaviors in which each successive behavior is *more intense* than the previous behavior.

3. *Behavioral defusion* is the process where a student engages in a series of behaviors in which each successive behavior is *less intense* than the previous behavior.

4. The process of defusion should inform teachers that the student is making positive progress. Even though the student may not have achieved the desired behavioral level, he or she is headed in the desired direction, which must be acknowledged, otherwise the student's behavior may escalate.

---

## KEY PRINCIPLE FOUR: NATURE OF BEHAVIORAL CHAINS

Behavioral chains consist of a series of discrete behaviors with each step in the chain prompting the next step. Many classroom activities can be described as behavioral chains or routines. For example, the students are asked to get ready to go to the library. This direction prompts students to finish up what they are doing, put their materials away, push in their chair, and line up at the door. Or, a teacher may tell the class to turn in their reports by next Tuesday, which requires the students to read the correct passages, make summary notes, take their textbook and notebook home, write the report from their summary notes, and turn in the report by Tuesday of next week.

In this book, behavior chains are referred to in the context of social behaviors, particularly for escalating behavior chains. The following illustration of an office referral is used to identify the key principles involved in understanding the nature of behavior chains and areas where interventions may be successfully applied. An incident report submitted by a teacher follows.

*Marietta was sitting at her desk with a bad attitude and was not doing her work. She was given a reminder to get started. She then started arguing about the work, and I tried to give her explanations and offered to help. She would not quit arguing, so I gave her the choice of doing the work now or after school. She became belligerent and began shouting. I gave her a warning to settle down, or she'd have to go to the office. She threw her books on the floor and stood up. I directed her to the office and she swung her arm and could have hit me in the face. I then called security.*

The behavior chain for the student based on information in this incident report consists of a series of discrete behaviors of increasing intensity in this order:

1. Sitting, not beginning the designated work, and displaying a negative attitude

2. Arguing

3. Continuing to argue

4. Displaying belligerence and shouting

5. Throwing materials and standing

6. Swinging her arm toward the teacher

The administrator who dealt with this incident was basically bound to address the most serious behavior first, the student swinging her arm and nearly hitting the teacher. The student may have been required to receive some counseling, and consequences typically would have been delivered, such as suspension, detention, and parent conference. Hopefully, these interventions had the desired effect of averting future occurrences of the behavior of aggression by swinging her arm toward the teacher. However, by focusing *only* on the last behavior of the chain, even though it was the most serious one, other behaviors in the chain were not addressed. This means that these behaviors were more than likely to recur in the classroom. To effectively address these behaviors earlier in the chain, all of which are undesirable and counterproductive for teaching and learning, a more detailed analysis of the behavioral chain is needed.

## Analysis of Behavioral Chains—Interaction Pathways

At first glance, the responses made by the teacher appear reasonable and normally would not result in a major incident, as in this case. The information provided in this incident report was restricted to the student's successive behaviors. There was no information at all on what may have prompted or set off each of these student behaviors. The assumption was that each student behavior in itself set the occasion for the next behavior, ultimately resulting in a serious act of swinging her arm toward the teacher's head. Behavior chains typically do not function this way. Additional stimuli or prompts are usually present, which set the occasion for the student's next behavior in the chain.

In many of these classroom situations, we are really looking at a *series of interactions* involving *both* teacher behavior and student behavior (or teacher–student interactions). For each student behavior, there is a corresponding or reciprocal teacher behavior. Each successive student behavior is *preceded* by a specific teacher behavior. Also, it could be argued, each teacher behavior is preceded by a specific student behavior. In this sense, we may conclude that the teacher behavior may have set the stage for the next student behavior and that the student behavior set the stage for the next teacher behavior. These successive interactions will be referred to throughout this book as an *interaction pathway*.

### Interaction Pathway Illustration

Suppose the incident report cited above was rewritten with the following information:

*Marietta was sitting at her desk, looking subdued, and was not doing her work. The teacher approached her, telling her that it was time to get started on her work. Marietta said she had finished it. The teacher noted that she had barely started and that if she needed help she could ask for it, otherwise she needed to get started. Marietta stoutly said she had done what was asked. The teacher pointed out Marietta needed to do 10 problems, and she had completed only 2, to which Marietta shouted, "No way. I am not doing this twice. That's not fair." The teacher told her to settle down and gave her the choice of doing her work now or doing it during the break. Marietta pushed her books on the floor and stood up. The teacher told her she needs to go to the office and nudged her arm toward the office. . Marietta vigorously swung her arm backward and nearly hit the teacher's head.*

While this report describes the same student behaviors as the initial incident report, the biggest difference is that the teacher responses are also included. The situation can now be described in terms of an *interaction-pathway diagram,* which depicts the successive teacher–student responses (Figure 1.1).

The pathway described in Figure 1.1 permits a close examination of the student's behavior in relation to the teacher's successive responses. Here is the key: One effective way of changing the student's successive behaviors in this example is to change the teacher's responses. Suppose, for example, the teacher's first response was along empathetic lines in recognizing that the student is bothered over something with a statement like, "Are you doing OK?" or, "Would you like a little time? And, I'll be back shortly." Similarly, when the student continued to argue, rather than confront the student, suppose the teacher disengaged, saying, "Why don't you try to continue, and I'll be back in a second." The teacher would then go to other students and return shortly. It is also clear in one of the last interactions of the pathway interactions that the teacher's nudge, physical contact, directing the student to go to the office was a powerful stimulus for the student to react physically. While there are several variations in responses the teacher could have made, the crucial point is that each teacher response sets the occasion for the student's next response. Basically, the teacher's response, in a large measure, *determines* what the student may do next. This means that the situation can be escalated or defused depending on the kind of response the teacher makes.

Another critical element of interaction pathways is that the teacher's responses serve to *reinforce* each student response. In the example above, by stopping work the student is successful in bringing the teacher to her and engaging in a discussion. The teacher coming to the student and prompting her to work reinforces the student stopping work. This response from the teacher also functions as a stimulus for the student's next response of arguing. In effect, each teacher response serves a *dual* purpose in the interaction pathway:

1. To reinforce the student's prior response in the chain; and

2. To set the occasion for the student's next response in the chain (Cooper, Heron, & Heward, 2007).

This dual function of teacher responses has three important implications:

1. It provides an explanation of how interaction pathways get established and maintained in the classroom. Once the pathway is established, the successive teacher and student behaviors become predictable.

**Figure 1.1**    Interaction-Pathway Diagram

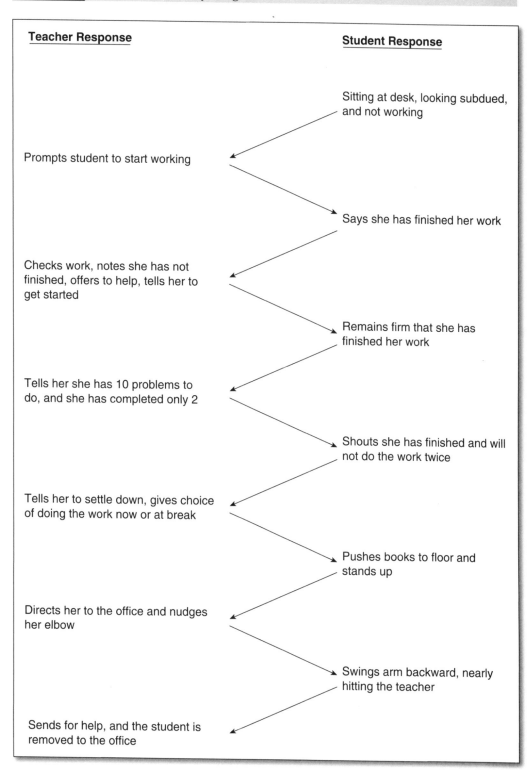

**Teacher Response**

Prompts student to start working

Checks work, notes she has not finished, offers to help, tells her to get started

Tells her she has 10 problems to do, and she has completed only 2

Tells her to settle down, gives choice of doing the work now or at break

Directs her to the office and nudges her elbow

Sends for help, and the student is removed to the office

**Student Response**

Sitting at desk, looking subdued, and not working

Says she has finished her work

Remains firm that she has finished her work

Shouts she has finished and will not do the work twice

Pushes books to floor and stands up

Swings arm backward, nearly hitting the teacher

2. It also provides direction for strategies to break up a problem pathway and redirect to an acceptable pathway. By changing the teacher's response, the student's behavior may not be reinforced (leading to extinction), and there is a different cue for the student's next behavior. This means a new, acceptable pathway of behavior may be developed.

3. If the teacher's initial response to the student's first behavior in the chain is changed, then the problem pathway may not even get started.

This book is designed to apply this *interaction-pathway analysis* to common problem behaviors students may exhibit in the classroom. The key is understanding that the teacher's responses reinforce the student behaviors and also set the occasion for the student's subsequent behaviors, which means that the student's behavior can be managed as a function of how the teacher responds to the problem behavior.

## Behavioral-Chain Patterns

Teachers often report student problem behavior as a predictable behavior chain. For example a teacher reports, "As soon as Jamie starts whining and complaining, I know there is going to be a blowup before long." Another teacher, speaking of a student with severe disabilities, said, "Once he starts tapping his fingers on the desk, it won't be long before he starts to slap his face and pull his hair." Similarly, a teacher remarked, "When Cerise stops working, stands up and walks around the room, she will soon become abusive to other students and me." In each of these examples, the teacher identified a behavior pattern in which certain student behaviors are followed by predictable, more-serious behaviors.

While it is quite helpful to be able to identify the successive behaviors of a student in a behavioral-chain pattern, it is *very important* to identify the reciprocal responses, especially from the teacher, to these behaviors. For example, when Jamie starts whining, what is the teacher's response to the whining? It is likely that the teacher's response is also predictable for the student, which will ensure completion of the chain (the student blows up). When the teacher responses to the student behaviors early in the chain are identified, the teacher is then in a stronger position to make changes in these responses that may break up the problem-behavior chain and replace it with acceptable patterns and routines. More details will be provided on this approach in Chapters 2 through 6.

Questions that often arise regarding behavioral-change patterns are, "How do these patterns get established in the first place?" and, "How are they maintained?" Clearly, these questions need to be answered if the problem behavior is to be effectively addressed and changed.

*Establishing Behavioral-Chain Patterns*

Behavior chains become established as patterns simply through the power of the reinforcing events that occur at the end of the chain. For example, suppose Marietta in the example above has a strong aversion to math. So when math is introduced, she begins to whine and complain. The teacher may address the whining, which leads to arguing and refusal from the student. The teacher then gives an ultimatum that the work needs to be done, help will be provided if need be, or Marietta will have to do it after school. Marietta then throws a tantrum, shouting and running around the room (she blows up). The teacher and teacher assistant then escort her to the time-out area to calm down. Marietta has now been successful in removing or avoiding the need to do math (at least in the short term). Task avoidance is a very common reason why students exhibit problem behavior, and when the students are removed from the situation because of escalating behavior, their behavior is reinforced. The whole chain is reinforced.

*Maintaining Behavioral-Chain Patterns*

The behavioral-chain pattern is maintained because the reinforcers for the last behavior in the chain continue to be applied or available to the student. In Marietta's case, when she blows up she is removed (this is her desired outcome). Moreover, the teacher and teacher assistant's behavior are also reinforced because they are effective in quieting the student, restoring order in the room, and enabling instructional activities to resume. Consequently, it is predictable that when Marietta begins to whine she will end up in the time-out area, removed from math. It is also predictable for Marietta that when she whines, the teaching staff will become engaged, ultimately removing her from the instructional activity.

One final property of behavioral chains is the relative strengths for each of the behaviors within the chain. Research on behavior chains has demonstrated that the behaviors at the end of the chain are the strongest because of their closest proximity to the reinforcing events; similarly, the behaviors early in the chain are weakest because of their relative distance from these reinforcers (Bellamy, Horner, & Inman, 1979; Cooper, Heron, & Heward, 2007; Watson & Butler, 2005). The implication is that interventions designed to address behaviors early in the chain are more likely to be successful compared to interventions for behaviors at the end of the chain. However, common practice often requires educators to target behaviors at the end of the chain because of their relative seriousness or intensity. The guiding rule is to intervene as early in the chain as possible.

The key points regarding the nature of behavioral chains are listed in Box 1.4.

**BOX 1.4**
**Key Properties of Behavioral Chains**

1. Behavioral chains consist of a series of discrete behaviors.

2. Behavioral chains often reflect escalation where each successive behavior is more serious than the preceding behaviors in the chain.

3. Addressing the last behavior in the chain may not change the behaviors early in the chain.

4. Each behavior in a chain is preceded by a stimulus that is usually the response from the teacher in classroom situations.

5. Behavioral chains can be perceived as *interaction pathways*, which involve successive responses from the student and teacher. The student's response sets the occasion for the teacher's response, and the teacher's response sets the occasion for the student's next response.

6. Behavioral chains are established and maintained by the presence of strong reinforcing events at the end of the chain. These events reinforce the entire chain.

7. The behavior at the end of a chain is strongest compared to behaviors early in the chain, which means that interventions are more likely to be effective when behaviors early in the chain are targeted.

## KEY PRINCIPLE FIVE: THE ROLE OF BEHAVIORAL EXTINCTION AND EXTINCTION BURSTS

### Behavioral Extinction

Teachers and behavior specialists need to have a good working understanding of the concept of extinction. *Extinction* refers to the process of systematically removing events that reinforce a behavior. For example, a student may act out in the classroom so as to be sent home. Once at home, the student has uninterrupted time for TV, cell phone use, and contact with other students who may be suspended, skipped school, or using their cell phones at school. Access to these preferred activities serve to reinforce the student's acting-out behavior in the classroom. However, if it was set up that on the next occasion when the student acted out in class he was sent to an alternative classroom, then the student would not have access to the reinforcing activities available at home. The student's acting-out behavior in class would be put to *extinction* by removing access to the reinforcers available at his home.

Similarly, the student who talks out a lot in the classroom is successful in obtaining a response from someone (either the teacher or other students). The teacher determines that the student's talking-out behavior is reinforced and maintained when others (teacher and students) respond to her. The teacher spends time explaining to the class that there is a classroom expectation that if you have something to say you need to raise your hand first. Also, the class may respond to students who raise their hand and are called on to respond. If someone does talk without raising his or her hand, then the class should not respond. The teacher also makes a concerted effort to encourage hand raising and not to respond to anyone who does not raise a hand, especially the targeted student. With this plan, the student's talking-out behavior was put to *extinction* by removing the reinforcers (responses from the teacher and other students).

The overall approach in using the extinction process is to identify events or responses that are reinforcing the problem behavior and then make adjustments so that these reinforcers are not available following the problem behavior. It is also presumed that the teacher would include in the plan strategies so that the student can access these reinforcers by following expected behavior (given the reinforcers are acceptable). For example, the student above received teacher and class attention for talking out. Once a plan was in place to remove attention for talking out, the student was able to receive attention by raising her hand. By following the expected behavior, the student was able to access attention.

## Extinction Bursts

One aspect of the extinction process that can be quite daunting and perhaps discouraging for teachers is the behavioral phenomenon of an extinction burst. When students become accustomed to accessing reinforcing events through problem behavior, they usually will exhibit more serious behavior when these reinforcers are removed. Their behavior may escalate. This escalation of behavior is known as an *extinction burst*. A teacher who has not worked with students with well-established behavior may misinterpret this escalation of behavior as an indication that the plan is not working. The teacher may say, "The plan is not working because the student is showing worse behavior now." In the illustration above, the student who went to the alternative classroom instead of being sent home may very well act out at in this classroom much more severely than in the initial classroom. Similarly, the student who talked out in class when she found no one was responding to her may talk out more often or may begin to shout. The student is basically communicating, "Hey, try ignoring this," and exhibits more intense behavior. The most serious outcome is that, if the student is successful in obtaining the desired reinforcers following an extinction burst, then the system has shaped a more serious problem. The student is more likely to exhibit this higher-intensity behavior in future. However, if teachers and program planners understand that an extinction burst is likely, supports can be put in place to manage the escalated behavior on a short-term basis. If the escalated behavior is not reinforced, it will extinguish quite quickly (Cooper, Heron, & Heward, 2007; Teachman & Smith-Janik, 2005).

More details will be provided on the extinction process and managing extinction bursts in Chapters 2 through 6, when common classroom problems are addressed. A summary of the key points on extinction is presented in Box 1.5.

---

### BOX 1.5
### Key Points of the Extinction Process and Extinction Bursts

1. *Extinction* refers to the process of removing the reinforcers that maintain a target behavior.

2. If the reinforcers are appropriate, students need to be taught how to access them through behaviors that are acceptable.

3. Once the extinction process is implemented, students are likely to exhibit more-serious behaviors, called *extinction bursts.*

4. Great care and planning needs to occur so that the students do not access the reinforcers following an extinction burst, otherwise the escalated behavior will become part of the student's repertoire.

5. Extinction bursts, if managed effectively, are usually of short duration.

---

## KEY PRINCIPLE SIX: THE POWER OF PERSONAL REACTIONS

Many teachers have experienced the situation where they have read a book or attended a workshop, and the information presented makes good sense and should be a routine practice. However, in the heat of the moment, the teacher may react and respond quite differently. For example, when a student becomes argumentative and disrespectful, it makes sense to withdraw, go to other students, and then return to the involved student and address the problem in a composed, matter-of-fact, and focused manner. However, in an actual moment, when the student becomes argumentative and calls the teacher an offensive name, the teacher may take exception to the name calling, approach the student immediately, and state in a somewhat upset manner, "That is no way to talk in here. You need to take yourself to the office." The student then utters a stream of language and makes a threat. In this instance, the teacher reacted personally to the offensive remark and confronted the student. The student then reacted with worse behavior. Clearly, the student's behavior was unacceptable and needs to be addressed, but reacting personally to the behavior exacerbated the problem. The issue becomes how to effectively address these kinds of behaviors and avoid escalating the student's behavior. The key point is for teachers not to react personally, as a necessary first step.

There are many reasons why teachers may react to certain student problem behaviors, lose composure to some extent, and respond in a way that accelerates the student behavior. These reasons could be culturally based. For example, the students may use language that is offensive to the teacher's values. Another common reason relates to authority. Teachers may feel their authority in the classroom is threatened or usurped by the challenging behavior from their students. Consequently, they may respond in a way to try to establish their authority, which can easily degenerate into an escalating power struggle. Finally, some students make it their business to press their teachers' buttons. These students know what behaviors are very likely to annoy or engage their teachers. Consequently, when the teacher becomes engaged, successive interactions occur, leading to more-serious problem behavior.

In general, when teachers take student behavior personally and react, their behavior is likely to escalate the student's behavior. The features of reactive behavior from teachers that are likely to escalate the student's behavior include immediacy of response, voice volume, tone of voice, body language, proximity to students, finger pointing, and perhaps threats. These factors will be more fully addressed in Chapter 4, Defusing Disrespectful Behavior, and Chapter 5, Defusing Agitation. The key points regarding personal reactions to problem behavior are listed in Box 1.6.

---

### BOX 1.6
### Key Points for Responding Personally to Problem Behavior

1. Sometimes, teachers take student behaviors personally and react in a way that escalates the student behavior.

2. There are occasions when teachers abandon logical or best-practice responses they might otherwise use when they are calm because they take certain behaviors personally.

3. Reasons for teachers taking student problem behavior personally are typically cultural or value based, related to authority questions, or to students knowing how to press their teachers' buttons.

4. Reacting personally to student behavior is usually manifest in teacher responses related to immediacy of response, voice volume, tone of voice, body language, proximity to students, finger pointing, and perhaps threats.

5. There is clearly a need to address these problem student behaviors in ways that are effective and at the same time not escalate the student behavior by not taking the behaviors personally.

## KEY PRINCIPLE SEVEN: ESTABLISHING FLUENT RESPONSES

Perhaps the biggest challenge to teachers in managing their initial responses to problem behavior is fluency. *Fluency,* in this book, refers to the degree to which a teacher responds in a planned way, automatically and smoothly, to certain situations. For example, consider the case where most of the class is on task with the class activity except for two students who are engaged in a side conversation. The desired first response from the teacher is to respond to the students who are on task and ignore the students who are off task. The first teacher notices the two students off task, immediately and naturally responds to the students who are on task with a brief compliment. This teacher's response is said to be fluent. A second teacher understands that it is better to respond to students on task, however, when confronted with this situation involving two students talking, the teacher hesitates, looks at the two students, looks at the rest of the class and in a delayed and awkward manner acknowledges the rest of the class who are on task. In this case, the teacher's response, although correct eventually, is not fluent. A third teacher, who also accepts that it is better to acknowledge the students who are on task as an initial response, in this situation, automatically addresses the two students who are off task. These three teachers showed the full range of application regarding fluency. The first teacher's response was marked with high fluency; the second teacher with low fluency; and the third teacher made the wrong response, responding with zero fluency.

It is possible for teachers to understand and agree with alternative approaches to managing behavior. They appreciate the logic behind the strategies and acknowledge the research on the effectiveness. However, when a targeted situation arises, they automatically respond in their old ways.

The root challenge, in these cases, is that teachers are required to change their behavior, specifically, to change their first response to situations where problem behavior occurs. This change is difficult and challenging for many teachers because, through repeated practice, they have become fluent with less-effective strategies. Consequently, even though willing to change, they automatically respond with their former strategies when problem situations arise. The challenge is to develop procedures to assist teachers to let go of existing habitual practices and become fluent with new and more-effective practices.

The most crucial response for teachers facing problem behavior, in many cases, is their *very first one.* This initial response from the teacher may elicit a planned or conditioned direct response from the student. Some students exhibit problem behavior expecting the teacher to respond in a predictable manner. Consequently, when the teacher responds in this way, the student automatically responds further involving more problem behavior or escalated behavior. By changing the teacher's initial response, the effect will often alter the student's subsequent responses, paving the way for defusing the situation and redirecting the student to appropriate behavior.

In each of the following chapters where specific problem behaviors will be addressed, procedures will be described for addressing this very crucial topic of achieving teacher fluency in response to problem behaviors. In addition, the section on strategies for defusing problem behavior in each chapter begins with a reiteration of this central approach of controlling the teacher's *initial* response. The key principles related to fluency are summarized on Box 1.7.

---

**BOX 1.7**
**Key Points for Establishing Fluent Responses to Problem Behavior**

1. *Fluency* refers to the degree to which a teacher responds in a planned way, automatically and smoothly, to certain situations.

2. Teachers may fully agree, either through research or demonstrations, that there are more-productive strategies for addressing problem behavior but have difficulty changing their responses.

3. Teachers, through repeated practice, are often quite fluent in using practices that are not very effective.

4. The core challenge comes in helping teachers to let go of their former practices and adopt different practices that have demonstrated effectiveness.

5. The most challenging response for teachers in obtaining fluency is their very first response.

6. Specific procedures are described in Chapters 2 through 6 for developing fluency with strategies for addressing common classroom problem behaviors, defusing the situations, and redirecting the students to appropriate behavior.

---

## CHAPTER SUMMARY

The bulk of strategies for addressing problem behavior in the classroom are designed to manage antecedent factors or proactive approaches and to manage consequences and follow-up procedures. Another important window for addressing problem behavior is the moment *immediately* following the occurrence of the initial problem behavior or the onset of the problem behavior. Specifically, the teacher's first response to the initial problem behavior can determine whether the behavior is defused and the classroom activities resumed or whether the problem behavior persists or escalates, and the classroom instruction interrupted.

A key to managing initial responses to student behavior is to properly understand *interaction pathways*. This concept is defined in terms of successive responses between the teacher and the student. One pathway may result in the student exhibiting more and more serious behavior as the interactions proceed. Another pathway may result in defusing the problem behavior, resulting in the student displaying acceptable behavior. This book is designed to utilize sound behavioral principles so that common classroom problem behaviors result in interaction pathways leading to acceptable behavior.

# 2

## *Defusing Off-Task Behavior*

Two of the most essential expectations teachers have for their students are cooperation and on-task behavior (Colvin, 2009; Lane, Wehby, & Cooley, 2006; Sprick & Garrison, 2008). It is impossible to imagine how teachers can conduct the teaching–learning process for their students when students do not cooperate or are frequently off task. Normally, when students follow their teacher's directions, are on task, and productively engaged in the activities designed by their teacher, learning will occur. By contrast, if the students are not following directions, are off task, and not engaged in the class activities, the intended learning will not occur, and behavior problems often will arise.

## DESCRIPTION OF OFF-TASK BEHAVIOR

A task is any direction or activity requested by teachers requiring responses from students. For example, at the end of break time, the teacher asks the class to put their materials away and get ready for science. The required task is for the students to put away the materials they have been using during break, go to their desks, and get their materials ready for the science lesson. The students who engage in these steps are said to be *on task*. Some students may continue using the materials from break or become engaged with other materials. These students are said to be *off task*.

Similarly, a math teacher explains how to solve quadratic equations. The students are then asked to begin working problems on page 54 from their textbook. Most of the class open their books to page 54 and begin working on these math problems. These students are said to be on task. However, some students begin talking to each other about their weekend and laughing quietly. These students are off task.

In general, on-task behavior refers to the student behaviors that relate to following the teacher's directions and engaging in the specified classroom activities. By contrast, off-task behavior refers to any behavior in which the teacher directions are not followed and are not connected with engagement in and completion of the required tasks.

# PREREQUISITE CONDITIONS

It cannot be overstressed that the procedures presented in this chapter, and in this book, for defusing problem behavior, are not meant to take the place of time-tested effective instructional and management practices. Rather, these defusing practices are designed to be used in addition to these practices. For this reason, a number of prerequisite conditions need to be firmly in place for the defusing practices to have any chance of being effective. These prerequisite conditions relate to practices teachers engage in to ensure that students are *on task*, which, in turn, gives the teacher more chance to successfully address off-task · behavior. There are seven such prerequisites: (1) cooperation and on-task behavior are taught as classroom expectations, (2) students have the necessary skills, (3) transitions are carefully planned, (4) task requirements are clearly presented, (5) adequate time is allocated for task completion, (6) on-task direction is checked, and (7) procedures for requesting assistance are established. A checklist and action plan for these prerequisites, Form 2.1, is provided in this chapter and in Appendix A.

## Cooperation and On-Task Behavior
## Are Taught as Classroom Expectations

There has been a growing practice in classrooms, schools, and school districts, nationally and internationally, to emphasize proactive approaches for managing student behavior (Colvin, 2007; Office of Special Education and Supports, 2004; Sprick & Garrison, 2008). These practices focus on taking direct measures to teach and sustain student behavioral expectations. The overall emphasis is to teach and establish desirable behavior throughout the school.

To address off-task behavior in a proactive manner, teachers take deliberate steps to teach their students *cooperation and on-task behavior* as classroom expectations. The ideal is that these behaviors are established as a *norm* in the classroom. By contrast, off-task behavior becomes the exception, enabling teachers to deal with it swiftly and effectively.

## Students Have the Necessary Skills

Clearly, when students are expected to work on a task, they need to have the prerequisite skills to complete the task. If they have not mastered these skills, they will have trouble becoming engaged with the task and staying on task. Teachers need to be sure that students have mastery of the skills required for the task. Ongoing assessment of skills—formative evaluation—should be a standard teacher practice (March & Peters, 2007; Stiggins, Arter, Chappuis, & Chappuis, 2007).

## Transitions Are Carefully Planned

Students often show off-task behavior at the beginning of a lesson. One explanation is that they are transitioning from one subject or period to another, which typically involves movement within the classroom or between classrooms; change of materials; change of activities; and, frequently, a change of teacher. These transitions can become quite distracting for some students and can set the occasion for problem behavior if they are not carefully planned and supervised. Behavioral expectations and routines should be established with the students for transitions so that when they enter the next lesson they are reasonably focused and can respond appropriately to the teacher (Evertson, Emmer, Clements, & Worsham, 1994; Weinstein & Mignano, 2003).

## Task Requirements Are Clearly Presented

If students are not quite clear on the tasks that they are being asked to do or cannot follow the directions, they will very likely exhibit off-task behavior. Teachers must ensure that their directions are clear and that the students know exactly what is required of them. Shores, Gunter, and Jack (1993), in a revealing study, showed that less than 20% of teacher directives to students with and without disabilities were preceded with information that would enable the students to respond correctly. Some students, if they do not understand the directions or task requirements, will ask for help or check with other students who know what is required. There are other students, however, who will soon display off-task behavior if they are unclear on what is required. While teachers may believe they are clear with directions and task requirements, it is imperative for them to take concrete steps to check for understanding, such as asking additional questions or calling on students to repeat what they are being asked to do.

## Adequate Time Is Allocated for Task Completion

When teachers set a task for their students, they should have an idea of how long the task will take to complete. Granted, there is usually a range of ability with the class, so some students will finish the task before others. Given this range of ability, the teacher should indicate an exit task for those who finish early, otherwise problem behavior may arise in the so-called dead time. In addition, provision should be made for those who do not finish the task; otherwise, on the next occasion, they may not even try, or give up trying, and become off task if they sense they cannot finish.

## On-Task Direction Is Checked

Once the task requirements have been explained, it is most important for the teacher to quickly check for two responses from their students related to on-task behavior and engagement in activities related to the lesson activity. First, is a prompt start. If students start quickly, they are likely to become engaged with the activity and stay on task. By contrast, if they start slowly, they may become distracted and exhibit off-task behavior. Second, the on-task direction is understood correctly. Students may appear to be working or busy, but they may be off task by not doing what was intended by the teacher. The direction is not understood correctly. In these cases, some students may give up after a while and become off task if they are required to start again. Once the teacher has explained the task requirements and checked for understanding, the teacher needs to move around the room fairly quickly to check that the students have commenced promptly and are doing what is intended in the lesson. Sometimes, a teacher may do a spot check by interrupting the class briefly to ensure that everyone has started in the right direction. Some teachers call this procedure "checking that the students are on track."

## Procedures for Requesting Assistance Are Established

Given there is a range of ability levels among students in the class, and varying degrees of concentration skills, some students may run into difficulties after they have commenced working on a task. If there are no established ways for getting assistance, they will soon exhibit off-task behavior. Teachers are encouraged to establish classroom routines that include procedures for obtaining assistance during instruction, such as students asking other students, raising their hands to ask for help, or approaching the teacher (Colvin & Lazar, 1997; Sprick, Garrison, & Howard, 1998).

## CHECKLIST AND ACTION PLAN
## FOR PREREQUISITE CONDITIONS
## FOR OFF-TASK BEHAVIOR

Form 2.1, Prerequisite-Conditions Checklist and Action Plan for *Off-Task Behavior* (Appendix A), is designed to assist teachers in determining whether the seven prerequisite conditions identified in this section are adequately in place before off-task behavior is directly targeted. In the first part of the form, the responses to each item are simply "yes" or "no." If there is doubt for any item, or if the response is unknown, then the item should be recorded as a "no" and addressed in the action plan. The second part of the form is the action plan where the teacher identifies steps to be taken to address any item that is recorded as a "no" in the checklist.

## ILLUSTRATIONS FOR COMMON
## OFF-TASK BEHAVIOR, GRADES K–12

In this section, three illustrations are presented for kindergarten and elementary, secondary, and specialist classes in which students display off-task behavior (Boxes 2.1, 2.2, and 2.3, respectively; pages 31–35). In each example, a narrative description is provided with a corresponding depiction of an interaction pathway, analysis of teacher responses, and analysis of student responses. The analyses identify interactions and teacher responses that may have contributed to maintaining the off-task behavior or escalation of the problem. In the next section, defusing strategies for addressing off-task behavior are described, which will be applied to each of these three illustrations.

## DEFUSING STEPS FOR ADDRESSING
## OFF-TASK BEHAVIORS

The reader will notice that the strategies recommended throughout this book are designed to be implemented *at the very onset* of the problem behavior. Emphasis is placed on the initial responses by the teacher when the problem behaviors first occur.

Moreover, there are some *universal strategies* included in the steps for addressing the targeted problem behaviors, such as maintaining the flow of instruction and acknowledging the cooperative students as first responses. Slight variations of these strategies are described for defusing the specific problem behaviors in each chapter,

There are five steps for addressing off-task behavior: (1) assess the situation, (2) maintain the flow of instruction, (3) attend to on-task students,

(4) redirect off-task student(s), and (5) follow through based on student's response. A checklist and action plan for these steps is provided at the end of this section.

### Step 1: Assess the Situation

Two questions must be answered before the following defusing strategies can be implemented. First, have the prerequisite conditions been met? The checklist and action plan in the preceding section, Form 2.1, Prequisite Conditions Checklist and Action Plan for *Off-Task Behavior,* is designed to help answer this question and develop an intervention if needed.

---

**Form 2.1**   Prerequisite-Conditions Checklist and Action Plan for *Off-Task Behavior*

## Checklist for Off-Task Behavior

*Scoring Key*

YES   NO     1. Cooperation and on-task behavior are taught as classroom expectations

YES   NO     2. Students have the necessary skills

YES   NO     3. Transitions carefully planned

YES   NO     4. Task requirements clearly presented

YES   NO     5. Adequate time allocated for task completion

YES   NO     6. On-task direction checked (students are "on track")

YES   NO     7. Procedures for requesting assistance established

### Action Plan for Items Scored "NO"

_____

_____

_____

# BOX 2.1
## Off-Task Illustration at Kindergarten and Elementary Level

| Illustration | Interaction Pathway |
|---|---|

The teacher had just completed reading a short story to the class and asked the children to listen carefully. She told them they attended very well to the story, and now they had to take the piece of paper on their desks and make a drawing of something they liked in the story. The majority of the class took their piece of paper, picked up their crayon, and began to draw—except for Louise, who began to play with some toy in her desk. The teacher approached her and said, "It is not time to be playing with that now. Can you tell me what we are supposed to be doing?" Louise continued to play with the toy and shrugged her shoulders. The teacher said, "Listen carefully. On the piece of paper here draw something that you liked from the story." The teacher pulled away remarking that the student was not ready to draw. Louise continued to play with her toy.

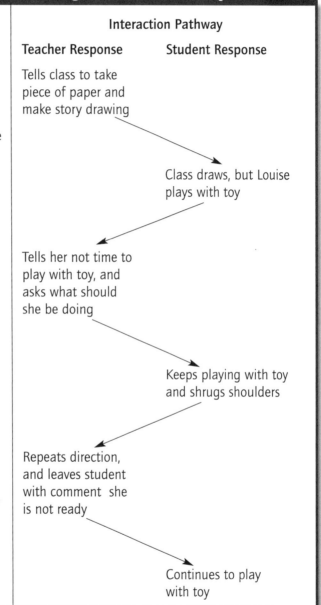

**Teacher Response**     **Student Response**

Tells class to take piece of paper and make story drawing

Class draws, but Louise plays with toy

Tells her not time to play with toy, and asks what should she be doing

Keeps playing with toy and shrugs shoulders

Repeats direction, and leaves student with comment she is not ready

Continues to play with toy

### Analysis of Teacher Responses to Off-Task Behavior

- The first student to receive teacher attention was the student who was off task.
- The first response from the teacher to this student was directed to the student's off-task behavior (playing with the toy).
- The teacher asked the student a question, leaving open the possibility for any response from the student.

- The teacher repeated the task direction and left the student in the off-task condition.
- The teacher made the comment that the student was not ready, which gave tacit permission to remain off task.

### Analysis of Student Responses for Off-Task Behavior

- The student secured teacher attention through off-task behavior.
- The student remained off task before the teacher came over, during conversation with the teacher, and after the teacher left.
- The student disrupted class to some extent.
- The student avoided the task and kept playing with her toy.
- The student is likely to repeat same behaviors in the near future.

## BOX 2.2
## Off-Task Illustration at Secondary Level

| Illustration | Interaction Pathway | |
|---|---|---|
| | **Teacher Response** | **Student Response** |

In the social studies class the students were writing a report on the Balkanization of Yugoslavia. Most of the students were writing or reading from their textbook. Two students were off-task, chatting to each other and laughing quietly. The teacher, Mr. Smith-White, spoke from the front of the room saying, "Joe, LaDelle, come on, it's time to get on with your reports." The two students looked at each other and a couple of other students turned around to look at them. The two students smiled, stopped talking, but made no effort to get started on the report. The teacher approached them and said, "I don't know if you heard me, but you need to get on with the report, otherwise you

Arranged class activity of report writing on Balkanization of Yugoslavia

Most students on task. Two students off task chatting and laughing

Publicly names and calls on the two students to begin work

Two students look at each other. Some students stop work and won't get it finished." One of the students said, "We are, but we're stuck." He looked at their notebooks and saw that they hadn't written anything. The teacher said, "You haven't even started." One student said, "I know, I just said we're stuck. We don't know what to do." The teacher said, "Well why didn't you raise your hand or come to me for assistance?" The student said, "I was going to, but you were busy." The teacher said "Enough," and he proceeded to explain what was required for the report.

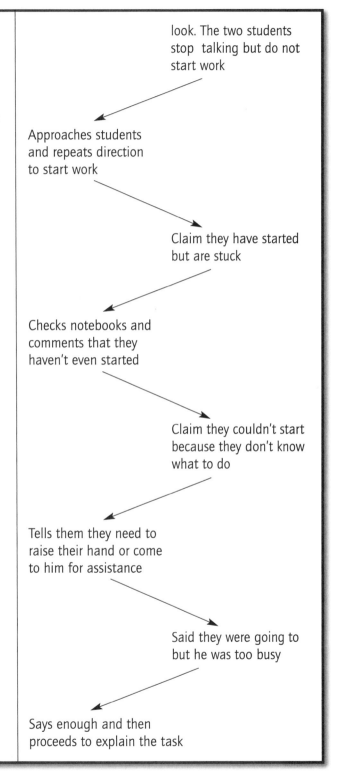

look. The two students stop  talking but do not start work

Approaches students and repeats direction to start work

Claim they have started but are stuck

Checks notebooks and comments that they haven't even started

Claim they couldn't start because they don't know what to do

Tells them they need to raise their hand or come to him for assistance

Said they were going to but he was too busy

Says enough and then proceeds to explain the task

## Analysis of Teacher Responses to Off-Task Behavior

- Responds to the students who are off task first
- Publicly names the students off task from the front of the room
- Engages with the students in a lengthy, back-and-forth discussion
- Ends up repeating the lesson directions and description of class routine for when students need help

## Analysis of Student Responses for Off-Task Behavior

- They are first to receive teacher attention in the class, delivered publicly, for being off task.
- Teacher moves to them providing personal attention.
- They interrupt some students causing them to stop and watch.
- They engage the teacher in a lengthy back-and-forth discussion.
- They perhaps annoy the teacher to some degree (when the teacher says "enough")
- They get assistance from the teacher without following the class routine for requesting assistance (raising their hand or approaching the teacher).
- They are highly likely to exhibit same behaviors in the future.

## BOX 2.3
## Off-Task Illustration in Specialist Class, Physical Education

| Illustration | Interaction Pathway | |
| --- | --- | --- |
| | **Teacher Response** | **Student Response** |
| The physical education class was in the gym engaged in a basketball drill where the students were placed in groups at each of the three basketball hoops. The students formed two lines at each hoop. The activity involved the front two students running to the hoop with one student passing the ball to the other one who tries to shoot the basket. They then pass the ball to the next two in line and the rotation continues. Two of the students, however, found an extra basketball and started passing it to each other, dribbling the ball while not | Gets basketball drill under way involving three stations and two lines of students per station | Class participates in drill except for two students, who started their own game with another ball |

participating in the group activity. The teacher blew his whistle and everyone stopped. The teacher then said, "Come over here quickly," to the two playing on the side. "What's going on here? You need to be in line working on your dribbling and shooting skills." One of the students said that it was boring, and the other said, "You don't get the ball much." The teacher said, "It's okay for the rest of the class, so you need to stand against the wall, till you are ready to join in." One student started to dribble the ball as he walked to the wall. The teacher said, "Give me the ball." The student rolled the ball toward the wall away from the teacher. The teacher sent the two students to the office for insubordination and disrupting the class and told the class to resume the drill.

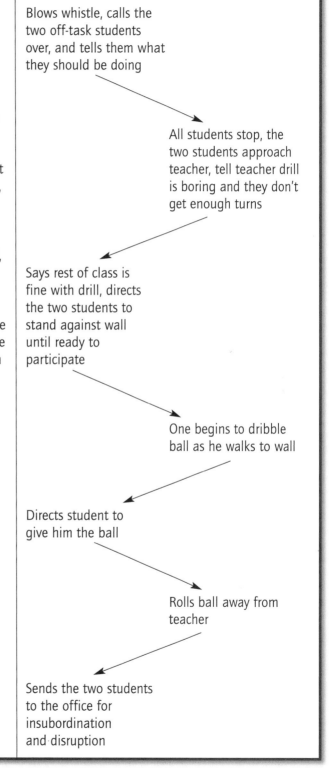

Blows whistle, calls the two off-task students over, and tells them what they should be doing

All students stop, the two students approach teacher, tell teacher drill is boring and they don't get enough turns

Says rest of class is fine with drill, directs the two students to stand against wall until ready to participate

One begins to dribble ball as he walks to wall

Directs student to give him the ball

Rolls ball away from teacher

Sends the two students to the office for insubordination and disruption

### Analysis of Teacher Responses to Off-Task Behavior

- The teacher stops all gym activity by blowing whistle.
- The teacher draws attention to the two students publicly (in front of whole class).
- The teacher gives the two off-task students his attention (again in front of whole class).
- The students are sent to the wall without a chance of joining the group (presumably for saying the class was boring).
- The teacher gives a direction (give me the ball) in the context of noncooperation.
- The teacher sends the students to the office for insubordination (even though the students were following the direction of going to the wall).
- The teacher sends both students to the office even though only one rolled the ball away from the teacher.

### Analysis of Student Responses for Off-Task Behavior

- The students drew attention from the teacher.
- The students disrupted the whole class.
- The students secured the attention of the whole class.
- The students were given opportunity to noncomply or make fun of the teacher in front of the whole class (saying the class is boring and rolling the ball away from the teacher).
- The students engaged the teacher in off-task behavior for a considerable amount of class time.
- The students were removed from class, which could please them as they did not to want to participate from the beginning of class.
- The students' behaviors were reinforced, and students were likely to repeat these or similar behaviors in the future.
- The students may hold a grudge against the teacher for dressing them down in front of their peers, which may set the occasion for further confrontation in subsequent lessons with this teacher.

The second question is how serious is the off-task behavior. Clearly, if the off-task behavior involves safety issues, such as a student throwing a chair across the room or threatening the teacher or other students, crisis or emergency procedures may need to be applied. Similarly, if the student's behavior is out of control and seriously disruptive, for example, a student running up and down the aisle of the classroom screaming and yelling profanities, emergency procedures need to be followed.

In this book, off-task behaviors refer to less-intensive situations, such as where the student may be talking to someone else instead of silently reading, out of seat and wandering around the classroom, just sitting at the desk staring at the floor, or engaged in some other activity not related to the lesson. In these cases, it is possible for the lesson to continue and for the teacher to defuse the off-task behavior in a systematic manner using the following steps.

**Note:** Readers needing additional information for addressing more-serious and pervasive behaviors are referred to these resources written by the author:

Colvin, G. (2004). *Managing the cycle of acting-out behavior in the classroom.* Eugene, OR: Behavior Associates.

Colvin, G. (2007). *7 steps for developing a proactive schoolwide discipline plan: A guide for principals and leadership teams.* Thousand Oaks, CA: Corwin.

Colvin, G. (2009). *Managing noncompliance and defiance in the classroom: A road map for teachers, specialists, and behavior support teams.* Thousand Oaks, CA: Corwin.

## Step 2: Maintain the Flow of Instruction

First and foremost, the teacher must make every effort to keep the lesson going in the *same direction* when off-task behavior occurs. If the lesson stops, or adjustments are immediately made, it is most likely that the student's off-task behavior will be reinforced. For example, the teacher is explaining something to the class and notices two students begin some side talk. The teacher *must continue* with the explanation and not stop or pause or stare at these two students. Business as usual has to be the first response from the teacher. If the teacher allows the lesson to be interrupted, then the two students talking are reinforced for their off-task behavior.

If the students cooperate and become engaged in the class activity, they should be acknowledged briefly. If students remain off task, the teacher would proceed to Step 3.

## Step 3: Attend to On-Task Students

Related to the strategy of maintaining the flow of instruction is the step of responding to the students who are on task (Step 3) and to delay responding to the students who are off task (Step 4). This order conveys to the class that teacher attention first goes to the students who are cooperating. The message is, "You want my attention, then you obtain it by following class expectations." An old behavioral adage is, "The behavior you attend to first is the first one you will get next time." In other words, the behavior the teacher attends to first is reinforced more strongly than the behavior the teacher attends to second.

This step of directly attending to the on-task students first is more effective with students whose off-task behavior is motivated by the need for attention. They learn that the surest way to secure their teacher's attention is to exhibit on-task behavior. However, if the student's off-task behavior is motivated by avoidance of the task, delaying responding to them will have little or no effect.

If the off-task students cooperate and become engaged in the class activity, they should be acknowledged briefly. If the students remain off task, the teacher would proceed to Step 4 where more direct approaches for addressing off-task behavior are applied.

## Step 4: Redirect Off-Task Students

An important consideration at this juncture is that the teacher has *delayed responding* to the off-task students by maintaining the flow of instruction (Step 2) and responding to the on-task students (Step 3). Given these students have not responded to these steps, the teacher now directly addresses their off-task behavior using a redirection strategy.

Redirection is a strategy teachers use to shift the students from what they are engaged in, off-task behavior, to what they should be engaged in, on-task behavior. The basic approach is to provide a direct cue or prompt to the off-task students on what the current task is for the class. The following details are suggested when providing redirection to off-task students:

- Go to the student and provide the redirection as privately as possible (as distinct from a public response in front of the class).
- Secure the student's attention in a respectful manner before delivering the redirection information. The student is already off task and may be fully attending to the off-task activity and not hear or receive the teacher's redirection.
- Minimize the attention given to the student with the redirection. It is best to use gestures such as pointing to a math book or whatever the current class activity is. Or, use brief language, such as, "It's math time. Let's go."
- Studiously avoid responding or drawing attention to the student's off-task behavior with comments such as, "You are not working," "You are out of your seat," or "You are reading when you should be writing." By responding directly to the off-task behavior, the teacher runs the risk of reinforcing these behaviors and of setting the stage for a counterproductive engagement with the students.
- Avoid asking questions such as, "What do you need to do?" or "What should you be doing now?" Questions also set the stage for further engagement and attention from the teacher. Attention needs to be minimal when the students are off task. In addition, a question enables the student to come up with an answer that may not be appropriate, and then the teacher has to deal with whatever response the student makes.

- Remind the student of the classroom procedures for seeking assistance or directly ask the student if he or she needs help with a comment, saying something such as, "Sarah, I can help you get started? Otherwise, let's get on with it, please." This step helps to rule out the possibility that the student may have difficulty in getting started.

**Note:** If the student needs help getting started, receives help, and stays on task, the teacher should approach the student later and remind him or her of the procedures for securing assistance. Otherwise, the student will learn that you get help and personal attention through off-task behavior.

### Step 5: Follow Through Based on Student's Response

If the student cooperates and becomes engaged in the class activity, he or she should be acknowledged briefly. The reason for a brief acknowledgment is that the reinforcement is delivered at the end of a chain of student behavior from off-task behavior to on-task behavior. If strong reinforcement is delivered, the teacher may strengthen the whole chain. The student may learn that positive teacher attention can be obtained by exhibiting off-task behavior first, followed by on-task behavior, whereas the students who are on task all of the time do not receive this level of attention. It is best to acknowledge students briefly when they resume on-task behavior and then reinforce these students a little more strongly later on when they have been on task for some time.

If a student remains off task, the teacher would move to the procedures described in Chapter 6 for addressing noncompliance and limit testing. At this juncture, the teacher has taken systematic steps to encourage the student to end off-task behavior and engage in the class activity, but the student persists with off-task behavior. Because the teacher, in Step 4, delivered a redirection to the student, which is really a direction, the student's refusal to resume the class activity can be determined to be noncompliant (given the student knows what to do and has the necessary skills). At this point, the teacher would move to strategies designed to address noncompliance and limit testing (described in detail in Chapter 6).

## CHECKLIST AND ACTION PLAN FOR DEFUSING OFF-TASK BEHAVIOR

The following checklist, Form 2.2, Checklist and Action Plan for Defusing *Off-Task Behavior* (Appendix B), is intended to be a resource for teachers so they can evaluate their responses to off-task behavior when it occurs. The intent is for teachers to self-evaluate their responses to off-task behavior, particularly to determine if they followed the recommended steps. For "yes" responses, the teacher is encouraged to maintain these responses consistently over time. Where "no" responses are recorded, the teacher is encouraged to develop an action plan to ensure the step is followed more reliably on the next occurrence of off-task behavior.

**Form 2.2**   Checklist and Action Plan for Defusing *Off-Task Behavior*

## Checklist for Defusing Off-Task Behavior

**Steps**

1. A quick assessment made on occurrence of off-task behavior to determine

| | | |
|---|---|---|
| a. Whether student has the prerequisite skills to complete the task | YES | NO |
| b. Whether off-task behavior was severe safety-wise or disruption-wise | YES | NO |
| If YES, crisis or emergency procedures followed | YES | NO |
| If NO, off-task defusing steps below followed | YES | NO |

| | | |
|---|---|---|
| 2. a. Flow of instruction maintained as a first response | YES | NO |
| b. Off-task students acknowledged briefly if on-task behavior followed | YES | NO |

| | | |
|---|---|---|
| 3. a. On-task students acknowledged as second response | YES | NO |
| b. No response made to off-task students | YES | NO |
| c. Off-task students acknowledged briefly if on-task behavior followed | YES | NO |

4. Redirection prompt was delivered as third response with features

| | | |
|---|---|---|
| a. Strong focus on required task | YES | NO |
| b. Brief language or use of gestures employed | YES | NO |
| c. No response made at all to student's off-task behavior | YES | NO |
| d. Remind student of procedures for assistance or offer to help | YES | NO |

| | | |
|---|---|---|
| 5. a. If student cooperates, displaying on-task behavior, brief acknowledgment is delivered | YES | NO |
| b. If student does not cooperate, move to procedures for noncompliance and limit testing from Chapter 6 | YES | NO |

### Action Plan (for Any Items Scored "NO")

_____

_____

_____

## APPLICATION OF DEFUSING STEPS TO THREE K–12 VIGNETTES FOR OFF-TASK BEHAVIOR

Earlier in this chapter, three vignettes were described for kindergarten and elementary, secondary, and specialist classes in which students displayed off-task behavior (Boxes 2.1, 2.2, and 2.3, respectively). In each case, the situations took a considerable amount of teacher time, in some cases the behavior worsened, and there was a strong likelihood that these or similar off-task behaviors would recur in the future.

In Boxes 2.4, 2.5, and 2.6 (pages 40–44), the sequence of events from each original illustration will be recalled followed by application of the steps recommended for defusing off-task behavior, enabling teachers to compare these interactions with those in the original vignette. Comments are also provided following each application of the defusing steps. For illustrative purposes, in the first case the student becomes on task after Step 3. In the second case, the students resume on-task behavior after Step 4. In the third case, the students remain off task through all four steps.

---

**BOX 2.4**
**Defusing Off-Task Behavior Vignette for**
**Kindergarden and Elementary Level**

### Original Illustration from Box 2.1: Off-Task Illustration at Kindergarten and Elementary Level

The teacher had just completed reading a short story to the class and asked the children to listen carefully. She told them they attended very well to the story, and now they had to take the piece of paper on their desk and make a drawing of something they liked in the story. The majority of the class took their piece of paper, picked up their crayon, and began to draw—except for Louise, who began to play with some toy in her desk. The teacher approached her and said, "It is not time to be playing with that now. Can you tell me what we are supposed to be doing?" Louise continued to play with the toy and shrugged her shoulders. The teacher said, "Listen carefully. On the piece of paper here draw something that you liked from the story." The teacher pulled away remarking that the student was not ready to draw. Louise continued playing with her toy.

### Recommended Defusing Steps for Managing Off-Task Behavior

**Step 1: Assess the Situation**

Teacher notices the student is off task, playing with a toy instead of coloring. Teacher determines that off-task behavior is not severe and that the student is capable of performing the requested task.

### Step 2: Maintain the Flow of Instruction

The teacher maintains the flow of instruction by asking if there are any questions and begins to move around the class, checking to see what the children are drawing.

### Step 3: Attend to On-Task Students

The teacher notices Louise is still off task, and with her back to Louise she acknowledges the class for starting their drawing saying, "Great. I appreciate how quickly you have started your drawing. Thank you."

Louise takes out her piece of paper and begins to draw. The teacher walks by her and reinforces her saying, "Good Louise, thanks for getting started," and moves to other students.

**Note:** In this case, the student responded to Steps 1 through 3 and switched to on-task behavior, which meant that the teacher did not need to apply Steps 4 and 5.

### Comments

1. The biggest difference in the two responses in this vignette of off-task behavior (Boxes 2.1 and 2.4) was the teacher's initial reaction. Initially, the teacher went immediately to the student who was off task (Box 2.1). By contrast, in the recommended response, Box 2.4, the teacher maintained instruction, responding to the class versus allowing instruction to be interrupted by going to the individual student who was off task.

2. Students who were on task received teacher attention first. The off-task behavior was put on extinction by delaying responding to the student.

3. The student who was off task did not receive teacher attention until she was on task.

---

**BOX 2.5**
**Defusing Off-Task Behavior Illustration for Secondary Level**

### Original Illustration from Box 2.2:
### Off-Task Illustration at Secondary Level

In the social studies class, the students were writing a report on the Balkanization of Yugoslavia. Most of the students were writing or reading from their textbook. Two students were off task, chatting to each other and laughing quietly. The teacher, Mr. Smith-White, spoke from the front of the room saying, "Joe, LaDelle, come on, it's time to get on with your reports." The two students looked at each other and a couple of other students turned around to look at them. The two students smiled, stopped talking, but made no effort to get started on the report. The teacher approached them and said, "I don't know if you heard me, but you need to get on with the report, otherwise you won't get it finished." One of the students said, "We are, but we're stuck." He looked at their notebooks and saw that they hadn't written anything. The teacher said, "You haven't even started." One student said, "I know, I just said we're stuck. We don't know what to do." The teacher said, "Well why didn't you raise your hand or come to me for assistance?" The student said, "I was going to, but you were busy." The teacher said, "Enough," and he proceeded to explain what was required for the report.

## Recommended Defusing Steps for Managing Off-Task Behavior

### Step 1: Assess the Situation

The teacher notices two students talking, laughing, and not under way with the report. He assesses the situation quickly, noting that the off-task behavior was not severe and that the two students were capable of performing the requested task based on their performance with other reports.

### Step 2: Maintain the Flow of Instruction

The teacher maintains the flow of instruction by moving around the classroom, looking at work, and reiterating the deadline for turning in the report.

### Step 3: Attend to On-Task Students

While noticing the two students are still talking and not under way with the report writing, the teacher looks at the rest of the class, commenting, "Good. Looks like we are well under way. Great start."

### Step 4: Redirect Off-Task Students

The teacher slowly approaches the two students who are off task, and points to their notebooks, saying, "Let's go. We don't have a lot of time. Do you need any help?" The two students open their notebooks and begin the report-writing work. The teacher says, "Thanks for getting under way," and moves to other students.

## Comments

1. Per the previous example, the first response from the teacher in the recommended procedures was to keep the lesson going as planned, maintaining the flow of instruction versus allowing the off-task behavior to interrupt the lesson plan.

2. Students who were on task received teacher attention first in the recommended procedures versus addressing the off-task students first. The students' off-task behavior was put on extinction by delaying a response to them.

3. When the teacher directly addressed the two students who were off task, the only focus was on getting started versus a sustained discussion, as in the initial vignette (Box 2.2).

## BOX 2.6
## Defusing Off-Task Behavior Illustration for
## Specialist Class, Physical Education

### Original Illustration from Box 2.3: Off-Task Illustration in Specialist Classes and Physical Education

The physical education class was in the gym engaged in a basketball drill where the students were placed in groups at each of the three basketball hoops. The students formed two lines at each hoop. The activity involved the front two students running to the hoop with one student passing the ball to the other one who tries to shoot the basket. They then pass the ball to the next two in line and the rotation continues. Two of the students, however, found an extra basketball and started passing it to each other, dribbling the ball while not participating in the group activity. The teacher blew his whistle and everyone stopped. The teacher then said, "Come over here quickly," to the two playing on the side. "What's going on here? You need to be in line working on your dribbling and shooting skills." One of the students said that it was boring, and the other said, "You don't get the ball much." The teacher said, "It's okay for the rest of the class, so you need to stand against the wall, until you are ready to join in." One student started to dribble the ball as he walked to the wall. The teacher said, "Give me the ball." The student rolled the ball toward the wall away from the teacher. The teacher sent the two students to the office for insubordination and disrupting the class and told the class to resume the drill.

### Recommended Defusing Steps for Managing Off-Task Behavior

#### Step 1: Assess the Situation

The teacher notices two students playing their own game and not joining the class activity. The teacher assesses the situation quickly, noting that the off-task behavior is not severe and that the two students are capable of performing the requested task based on their earlier performances in basketball activities and that it was easy for them to just follow what the other students were doing.

#### Step 2: Maintain the Flow of Instruction

The teacher maintains the flow of the lesson by moving to each station and commenting on execution and providing a few suggestions to some students regarding form.

#### Step 3: Attend to On-Task Students

While noticing the two students are still playing their own game on the side, the teacher looks to one of the groups and says, "This group here is doing a great job. Thanks for the hard work."

### Step 4: Redirect Off-Task Students

The teacher approaches the two students slowly, points to one of the stations, and says, "Let's go. Time to join in the game." The two students keep playing their game and do not join the group.

### Step 5: Follow Through Based on Students' Response

The teacher now regards their behavior as noncompliant or testing limits and follows the procedures identified in Chapter 6 for defusing noncompliance and limit testing.

### Comments

1. Even though the steps used through Step 4 were unsuccessful in getting the two students to participate in the class activity, the teacher was able to maintain the class activity for the remainder of the period without student interruption.

2. By using these steps, the teacher was able to avoid the ongoing interactions resulting in disrespectful and confrontational behavior present in the original vignette. Escalation was avoided.

3. The strategies used for addressing noncompliant behavior in Chapter 6 are much more likely to be successful given that the steps above were followed, and the student behavior had not escalated.

## CHAPTER SUMMARY

Off-task behavior is a very common problem behavior in classrooms. Unless these behaviors are managed effectively and efficiently, learning opportunities may be lost. In addition, it is always possible for even low-level off-task behavior to escalate to more-serious, disruptive, and unsafe behavior.

There are a number of prerequisite conditions that need to be in place before the recommended strategies for defusing off-task behavior should be applied. These prerequisite conditions include proactive classroom practices designed to establish a positive environment in the classroom to support desirable behavior and learning. Moreover, teachers need to be sure that the students who display off-task behavior understand what is required of them and are capable of performing the task. Form 2.1, Checklist and Action Plan for Task Prerequisite Conditions (Appendix A), is included to assist teachers in determining that the prerequisite conditions have been met.

The fundamental purpose in the strategies for addressing off-task behavior is for the teacher to delay responding to these behaviors. This delay is best accomplished by maintaining the flow of instruction and by acknowledging the students who are on task as the teacher's first responses. The remaining steps are designed to help the off-task students focus on what is required in the task, to provide assistance as appropriate to them, and, above all, to avoid unnecessary engagement with the students who are off task. If the students respond to these steps and become engaged in the required task, the teacher should acknowledge their cooperation. If they resist these steps and remain off task, the teacher would implement the strategies described in Chapter 6 for addressing noncompliance and limit testing. The steps for defusing off-task behavior are summarized as a checklist in Form 2.2, Checklist and Action Plan for Defusing *Off-Task Behavior* (Appendix B).

# 3

## *Defusing Rule Infractions*

It is impossible to imagine a teacher conducting a classroom without rules or expectations. These rules are designed to assist with the proper functioning of the classroom so that the teacher can teach and the students can learn. The simple fact is that a classroom consists of a relatively large number of people, with diverse needs and abilities, in a confined space. Rules and expectations are needed to establish the degree of organization necessary for all students to experience academic, social, and personal success in a safe, orderly, and positive environment.

One of the most interesting and encouraging trends over the past two decades in education has been the ongoing national and international focus on establishing positive, safe, and welcoming school and classroom environments (Colvin, 2007; Sprague & Golly, 2004; Sprick, Garrison, & Howard, 1998). A key component for accomplishing this goal has been to place a strong emphasis on establishing and maintaining schoolwide and classroom rules and expectations (Brophy, 1998; Metzler, Biglan, Rusby, & Sprague, 2001; Moran, Stobbe, Baron, Miller, & Moir, 2008).

When teachers and school personnel make a concerted effort to teach and establish schoolwide and classroom expectations, it can be expected that the vast majority of students will follow these rules and expectations. However, there will be some students who will not follow the rules occasionally, and a small number of students who will violate the rules on a regular basis.

# DESCRIPTION OF RULE INFRACTIONS

*Rule infractions* refer to those student behaviors that are in direct opposition to procedures established in the school and classroom. For example, the teacher has established a rule that when the students move around the classroom, they are to walk. A particular student runs in the classroom. The running would be considered a violation of the rule "walk in the classroom."

In order to establish classroom rules and, in particular, to defuse rule infractions, it is important to understand that there are three major variations of these rules: (1) school and classroom regulations, (2) routines, and (3) expectations.

### School and Classroom Regulations

*Regulations* refer to those very concrete behaviors that are required of all students to ensure particular outcomes for students and staff, such as *school safety* (speed limits in the student parking lot and keeping hands and feet to oneself in the hallways), *order* (using a reasonable voice level in the building or responding to bells and schedule demands), and *standards* (proper dress codes, use of proper language, and civility toward others). School and classroom regulations and appropriate rationales are typically listed in the school handbook and systematically communicated to the student body.

### Routines

Classroom routines are those common day-to-day procedures that are completed by students with minimum assistance from the teacher. Routines usually consist of a number of sequential behaviors tied to specific activities conducted in the classroom. For example, a teacher may expect the students to turn in completed assignments at a specific place in the room, return to their desk, and begin another activity without prompting from the teacher. Or, upon the teacher announcing to the class that it is time for P.E., the students follow the routine of putting their materials away in their desk, pushing in their chairs, lining up at the door, and waiting for the teacher's signal to move to the gym.

Establishing and maintaining classroom routines is a high-priority activity for all teachers, K–12. The routines will obviously vary from grade to grade; however, all teachers need effective routines for delivering instruction, organizing the various activities in a classroom, and managing behavior.

### Expectations

Classroom expectations are general principles or guidelines for student behavior, such as students are expected to "do their best."

Fulfilling this expectation will vary from student to student; for example, two students may do their best in a quiz while one of them scores higher than the other. Expectations may also show considerable variation in application from setting to setting. For example, an expectation may be to respect one another. To respect one another in the library could mean that students talk very quietly or not at all, whereas at recess respecting one another is not usually affected by voice level.

Perhaps one of the most undisputed beliefs regarding teaching and learning is the strong relationship between teacher expectations and student achievement and social behavior. Simply put, if the teacher expects the students to achieve and behave appropriately, they will. Conversely, if the teacher expects the students to achieve poorly and behave inappropriately, they will. However, since expectations are general in nature, as distinct from classroom regulations that are usually very concrete, teachers have to take considerable care in establishing and maintaining classroom expectations.

## PREREQUISITE CONDITIONS

As in the case for defusing off-task behavior in Chapter 2, it is particularly important to ensure that the following prerequisite conditions have been satisfied. The strategies designed to defuse rule infractions rest on the assumption that the teacher has made the determination that the student is fully aware of the rule and clearly breaks it. If there is any confusion or uncertainty regarding the rule then the teacher should clarify and teach the rule (rather than jump to strategies used to address breaking of the rule). Four prerequisite conditions relate to practices teachers conduct in order to ensure that students are quite cognizant of the rules that are operative in the classroom: (1) schoolwide rules are taught and established by faculty, (2) classroom rules and expectations are systematically taught, (3) students are frequently acknowledged for following the rules, and (4) practices are in place to monitor and review the rules. A checklist for these prerequisites is provided in this chapter.

### Rules Are Systematically Taught

The ideal situation is that a schoolwide effort, involving the entire faculty, is made to teach and sustain behavioral expectations that apply to all students and all settings (Liaupsin, 2005; Sprague & Golly, 2004). The classroom is then viewed as one of the school settings where these expectations are implemented, and teachers work together on the common behavioral goals for all students.

From the very first day of school, and throughout the school year, teachers must take definitive steps to teach and establish classroom rules (regulations, routines, and expectations). To establish classroom rules, teachers typically use similar strategies used to teach and establish learning and skill development in other areas, such as academics, music, art, physical education, and sports (Liaupsin, 2005; Sprick, Garrison, & Howard, 1998).

### Students Are Frequently Acknowledged for Following the Rules

Once the classroom rules and expectations have been taught and established, the next prerequisite condition is for the teacher to take steps to ensure that the behaviors are frequently reinforced and encouraged throughout the school year. The problem is that teachers and students become engaged in a whole variety of activities during the course of the year, resulting in some students forgetting the rules. Consequently, when the teacher addresses a student who may have broken a rule, the issue becomes clouded because the student may have forgotten the rule or is not fully aware of its importance.

Typically, teachers acknowledge cooperation with rules and expectations as an ongoing and integral part of a lesson or activity. In addition, many teachers have structured recognition plans in the classroom to acknowledge students who cooperate with the classroom rules. Students need to be fully aware of the school and classroom rules and need to be systematically reinforced and encouraged to keep the rules and exhibit expected behaviors throughout the school year.

### Practices Are in Place to Monitor and Review the Rules

As the year progresses, some rules need to be modified so that they are clearer and make more sense to students and teachers. To enable these modifications to occur, teachers should have a review system in place, usually based on data from office referrals and classroom data records, teacher observations, and feedback from students and other teachers. If the rules are inadequate or unclear, students may become confused. So when they break one of these rules, strategies used by the teacher based on the students knowing and understanding the rules are likely to become ineffective, unpopular, and probably unfair.

## CHECKLIST AND ACTION PLAN FOR PREQUISITE CONDITIONS FOR RULE INFRACTIONS

Form 3.1, Prerequisite-Conditions Checklist and Action Plan for *Rule Infractions* (Appendix C), is designed to assist teachers in determining whether the prerequisite conditions identified in this section are adequately in place before the problem of rule infractions is directly targeted.

**Form 3.1**   Prerequisite-Conditions Checklist and Action Plan for *Rule Infractions*

## Checklist for Rule Infractions

*Scoring Key*

YES     The item is clearly in place

NO      The item is not in place, or there is uncertainty whether it is in place
        or not

**Items**

YES   NO   1. Schoolwide rules taught and established by faculty

YES   NO   2. Classroom rules and expectations systematically taught

YES   NO   3. Students frequently acknowledged for following classroom rules

YES   NO   4. Practices in place to monitor and review the rules

### Action Plan for Items Scored "NO"

_____

_____

_____

# ILLUSTRATION FOR COMMON RULE INFRACTIONS

In the following illustration, Box 3.1, a narrative description of the problem is provided with a corresponding depiction of an interaction pathway, analysis of teacher responses, and analysis of student responses. The analysis of teacher responses indentifies interactions that may have contributed to maintaining the rule infraction or escalation of the situation. In the next section, recommended defusing steps for addressing rule infractions are described, which will be applied to this illustration and followed by a practice example at the end of the chapter.

## BOX 3.1
## Rule Infraction at Kindergarten and Elementary Level

### Illustration

Mrs. Jones-White has a rule in her classroom that students bring items to school that are for their work, or particular items for which they have obtained permission.

On this morning, Mrs. Jones-White notices that one student, Malika, has her head inside her desk for quite some time while the rest of the class is reading silently. She approaches the student and notices she is playing with a particular game. The teacher says, "You know better than that, Malika. You can't bring things like that to school." Malika says, "My parents gave it to me for my birthday." The teacher says, "Well, that's something you can have at home, then, but you still cannot have things in class without permission. So, you had better give it to me for now and collect it at the end of the day." Malika puts her head down and mumbles that it is not fair and holds the game more tightly. The teacher says, "Last chance, Malika. You either give me the game, or you will lose it." Malika starts crying.

### Interaction Pathway

**Teacher Response**

Notices student engaged with something inside her desk and finds it is a game. Tells student she should know better, and she has broken a rule

**Student Response**

Says her parents gave her the game for a birthday present

Tells her reason for having the game does not matter. Repeats the rule (must have permission for game). Directs student to give her the game

Puts head down, and hangs on to game

Gives ultimatum to hand over the game, or she will lose it

Student cries

### Analysis of Teacher Responses to Rule Infraction

- The first response is to give teacher attention to the student who was off task.
- This first response from the teacher to this student was directed to the student's off-task behavior of breaking a rule by playing with a game.
- The teacher used language that could be perceived as a put-down: "You know better than that."
- The teacher dismissed the student's remark about the item being a gift from her parents for her birthday, and, perhaps, ignored the occasion of it being the student's birthday.
- The teacher was insensitive to the value the gift may have for the student by demanding that she hand it over.
- The teacher cornered the student by making her choose between handing over the gift or losing it.

### Analysis of Student Responses for Rule Infraction

- The student secured teacher attention through playing with the game during silent reading (off-task behavior).
- The student considered breaking the rule of bringing unapproved items to school was not an issue because what she had was a birthday gift (implicit parental approval).
- The student disrupted class to some extent.
- The student avoided the task of silent reading and engaged in a preferred activity.
- The student was threatened with loss of her game or special birthday gift.
- The student became upset with tears over the possibility of losing her game.
- The student probably will bear a grudge against the teacher for being unfair (in the student's eyes).

## DEFUSING STEPS FOR ADDRESSING RULE INFRACTIONS

There are seven steps for defusing rule infractions in the classroom: (1) assess the situation, (2) maintain the flow of instruction, (3) attend to on-task students who are following the rules, (4) clarify the rule or expectation, (5) explicitly request the student to take care of the problem, (6) present problem-solving options if needed, and (7) follow through based on student's response.

### Step 1: Assess the Situation

Two questions must be addressed before the following defusing strategies are implemented. First, have the prerequisite conditions been met?

The checklist and action plan in the preceding section, Form 3.1, Prerequisite-Conditions Checklist and Action Plan for *Rule infractions,* is designed to help answer this question and develop an intervention if needed.

The second question is how serious is the rule infraction? The behavior may involve breaking a schoolwide rule, such as bringing a knife to the classroom or stealing money from another student. In these cases, all faculty are expected to follow standard procedures, such as making an office referral or using emergency procedures, depending on the particular infraction and schoolwide procedures.

In this book, rule infractions refer to the less-intensive problems that the teacher is expected to address within the classroom, such as situations where the student may help herself to supplies without permission, wear an inappropriate shirt, go to the front of the line instead of the end of the line as the class is getting ready for recess, chew gum, use a cell phone, or talk to someone during a quiz when silence is expected. In these cases, it is possible for the lesson to continue and for the teacher to address the rule infraction in a systematic manner (for more-intensive and pervasive problems, the reader is referred to Colvin, 2009; Sprick & Garrison, 2008).

### Step 2: Maintain the Flow of Instruction

First and foremost, the teacher must make every effort to maintain the lesson or activity as if the rule infraction had not occurred (again, presuming the behavior is one that the teacher is expected to manage). If the lesson stops, or adjustments are immediately made, it is most likely that the student's rule infraction behavior will be reinforced. For example, the teacher is explaining something to the class and notices a student make a move to use a cell phone. The teacher then stops the explanation and approaches the student. Interrupting the explanation and publicly approaching the student provides the student with a high level of attention, which may reinforce the rule infraction behavior. In addition, the student's behavior may escalate to save face because the whole class may be watching. The teacher *must continue* with the explanation and not stop, pause, or stare at the student using the cell phone. The teacher conducts business as usual as the *first* response and *delays* responding to the rule infraction.

### Step 3: Attend to On-Task Students
### Who Are Following the Rules

Related to the strategy of maintaining the flow of instruction is the step of responding to the students who are on task, minding the rules, and delaying a response to the student who is exhibiting a rule infraction. This order conveys to the class that teacher attention first goes to the students who are cooperating with the lesson activity and classroom rules. The message is, "You want my attention, then you obtain it by following class expectations." For example, the teacher has a rule or expectation that when the students finish they are to turn in their work and select a book from the shelf for some quiet reading time (to accommodate the different times it takes the students to finish the work).

The students follow this procedure except for Bree. Bree finishes her work but does not turn it in and, instead, rushes to the shelf to secure a popular book. The teacher moves around the class acknowledging the students who are working on their writing assignment and makes the statement, "I really appreciate the students who have turned in their work and are now reading quietly." The teacher then addresses Bree (as in the procedures for Step 4).

## Step 4: Clarify the Rule or Expectation

When addressing rule infractions, it is most important to ensure that the students know the rule. Consequently, when the teacher responds directly to the student who has exhibited the rule infraction, the initial intent is to clarify the rule. Typically, the teacher would take the student aside, or approach him or her as privately as possible, and *restate* the rule. For example, in the illustration in Step 3, the teacher might say to the student, "Bree, the procedure we have is to turn in your work first and *then* get something to read. The work has to be placed in the in-basket on my desk. Do you understand that?"

Some teachers, in this situation, like to ask questions such as, "Bree, what is the procedure when you finish your writing assignment?" This author's preference is to avoid questions, at least initially, otherwise the student may respond in ways that prolong engagement or the student behavior may escalate because he or she has been caught breaking the rule.

It is important to minimize the rule explanation because the student is receiving individual attention in class through breaking a rule. It may happen that the student may want to argue, discuss the rule more, or complain that the rule is not fair or ridiculous. If further time is needed, the teacher tells the student that they could get together later as the period ends, or some other time, to discuss the matter further. In this way, the student is not being denied the opportunity to clarify the rule further and the teacher does not become locked in with the student, providing additional attention, following the rule infraction.

## Step 5: Explicitly Request the Student to Take Care of the Problem

This particular step has to be carefully managed. The reason is that some students, when they break a rule, are exhibiting noncompliance and defiance. In this sense, the student may be challenging the teacher or at least exhibiting confrontational behavior. If the teacher becomes directive at this juncture, that is, in the context of noncompliance and defiance, the student is highly likely to react and may become belligerent and more defiant.

To prevent these situations, the teacher turns the responsibility back to the student and carefully avoids giving specific directions. For example, in the case of Bree in Step 4, who didn't follow the procedures for turning in work, the teacher would clarify the rule and then say something like, "Now Bree, please take care of this." Another student exhibits a dress code infraction by wearing a T-shirt that has a rude message. The teacher approaches him and says, "Andy, that shirt has a rude message, and our dress code says it can't be worn" (Step 3, rule clarification). "You'll have to take care of it." Similarly, Melissa has a cell phone on her desk. The teacher approaches her and privately says, "Melissa, we have a school rule that cell phones can't be seen in class" (Step 3, rule clarification). "I need you to deal with it, please." A final example shows Joey lined up for recess without putting things away from his desk. The teacher takes him aside and says, "Joey, we need to put things away on our desk before we line up" (Step 3 rule clarification). "So, take care of that please." In each of these examples, the teacher clarifies the rule then puts the responsibility back on the student to take care of the problem.

## Step 6: Present Problem-Solving Options If Needed

In some cases, it is quite straight forward what the student needs to do to address the rule infraction. For example, in Bree's case, all she needs to do is take her assignment to the teacher's desk and put it in the in-basket.

In other cases, the problem solving may require more thought. For example, the student who came to class wearing a rude T-shirt may not know what to do to address the situation, especially on the spur of the moment when there could be some aggravation or embarrassment. In these cases, the teacher provides some options. For example, in the case of the student involved with dress-code infraction, the teacher could say, "Look, you can get a shirt from the gym, turn yours inside out, or wear a jacket. It doesn't matter which one you choose as long as you take care of it."

It is also important for the teacher to present some options, as then there is less chance of the student being cornered and additional reactive behavior occurring. Moreover, the responsibility is still left to the student to select an option and solve the problem.

**Step 7: Follow Through Based on Student's Response**

If the student cooperates and takes acceptable action to solve the problem, he or she should be acknowledged briefly. The reason for a brief acknowledgment is that the student may be somewhat agitated because he or she had to back down and comply with the classroom rule or expectation. If strong reinforcement or overt attention is delivered, the student may perceive that the teacher is being condescending, rubbing it in, or communicating that the student has lost the power struggle, which may bring on resentment and further problem behavior.

Sometimes, it is desirable for the teacher to approach the student later at a more neutral time and acknowledge the choice made with a comment like, "Thanks for solving that problem. I expect it wasn't real easy for you, but I appreciate your cooperation."

If the student does not cooperate and refuses to select an option to solve the problem, the teacher would proceed to the procedures described in Chapter 6 for addressing noncompliance and limit testing. At this juncture, the teacher has taken systematic steps to encourage the student to cooperate and follow the classroom rule or expectations, but the student resists the problem-solving options. This sustained refusal to cooperate and take care of the rule infraction can be determined as noncompliance, so the teacher would then implement the procedures described in Chapter 6, Defusing Noncompliance and Limit Testing.

**Note:** While the teacher may hope the student will respond to these procedures, in some cases the students may simply be on a path where they won't respond, and the resistance will run its course. Regardless, the teacher follows through, and the next time around the student may cooperate. The power of these strategies to change behavior lies in consistency over time.

## CHECKLIST AND ACTION PLAN FOR DEFUSING RULE INFRACTIONS

Form 3.2, Checklist and Action Plan for Defusing *Rule Infractions* (Appendix D), is intended to be a resource for teachers, so they can evaluate their responses to how rule infractions are managed in the classroom. The intent is for teachers to self-evaluate their responses to rule infractions, particularly to determine if they followed the recommended steps. For "yes" responses, the teacher is encouraged to maintain these responses consistently over time. Where "no" responses are recorded, the teacher is encouraged to develop an action plan to ensure the step is followed more reliably on the next occurrence of a rule infraction.

**Form 3.2**    Checklist and Action Plan for Defusing *Rule Infractions*

## Checklist for Defusing Rule Infractions

**Steps**

1. A quick assessment made on occurrence of rule
   infraction to determine
   a. Whether student knows the rule or expectation                    YES    NO
      If NO, rule needs to be taught or clarified
   b. Whether the rule infraction was severe safety-wise or
      disruption-wise                                                  YES    NO
      If YES, crisis or emergency procedures followed                  YES    NO
      If NO, defusing steps below followed                             YES    NO

2. a. Flow of instruction maintained as a first response             YES    NO
   b. On-task students acknowledged                                   YES    NO

3. a. Students following rule acknowledged                           YES    NO
   b. No immediate response to student exhibiting rule infraction     YES    NO

4. Rule clarified and restated                                        YES    NO

5. Student directly asked to take care of the problem                 YES    NO

6. Options presented if student does nor (or cannot) initiate response  YES    NO

7. a. If student cooperates and addresses problem, brief
      acknowledgment delivered                                        YES    NO
   b. If student does not cooperate and refuses to address problem,
      procedures for noncompliance from Chapter 6 implemented         YES    NO

### Action Plan (for Any Items Scored "NO")

_____

_____

_____

_____

# APPLICATION OF DEFUSING STEPS TO AN ILLUSTRATION OF RULE INFRACTIONS

Earlier in this chapter, an illustration was described for kindergarten and elementary-aged students, Box 3.1, where a student broke a classroom rule. The situation took an unduly amount of teacher time, the student's behavior worsened, and there was a strong likelihood that these or similar rule infractions would occur again in the future. This example will now be revisited, and the steps recommended for defusing rule infractions will be applied (Box 3.2), followed by some comments.

---

## BOX 3.2
### Defusing Rule Infraction Illustration for Kindergarten and Elementary Student

### Recommended Defusing Steps for Managing Rule Infractions

#### Step 1: Assess the Situation

Mrs. Jones-White is reasonably certain that Malika knows the rule for what can be brought to class, as she went over this rule in the opening activity for class. She also concludes that the behavior is one she should deal with in the classroom.

#### Step 2: Maintain the Flow of Instruction

Mrs. Jones-White, aware that Malika is not reading but playing with something in her desk, moves around the class quietly acknowledging the students who are engaged in the class activity of silent reading, and she checks to see if anyone needs help.

#### Step 3: Attend to On-Task Students Who Are Following the Rules

In this example, only one student has broken the rule, while the rest of the class is engaged in the designated activity. The teacher acknowledges the on-task students and pays a special compliment to another student, Andrea, who usually has trouble with silent reading.

#### Step 4: Clarify the Rule or Expectation

The teacher approaches Malika and says quietly and privately, "Malika, it is time for reading, and remember our rule, you have to have permission to bring your special things to class. We talked about that this morning." Malika blurts out that her parents gave it to her for her birthday. The teacher calmly says, "Well, that is great you got a nice present for your birthday. But, you still need to get permission to bring your special things to class, and you haven't done that."

#### Step 5: Explicitly Request the Student to Take Care of the Problem

The teacher then says, "Malika, I want you to take care of this now please." Malika quickly says, "May I have this Bonzo game please?"

#### Step 6: Present Problem-Solving Options If Needed

The teacher says, "Yes, you need to get permission for the game. But, now is the time for reading. You can put the game up at my desk or in your locker, and see me before recess about permission."

**Step 7: Follow Through Based on Student's Response**

The student puts the game on the teacher's desk, returns to her desk, and begins reading. The teacher briefly thanks her for putting the game away and getting started with her reading.

**Comments**

1. The teacher delayed responding to the student who exhibited the rule infraction and as a first response acknowledged the students who were on task with the silent reading. She also paid more attention to one student, Andrea, who usually struggles with this activity (demonstrating that you get teacher attention when you make more effort to cooperate with the class activity).

2. The teacher clarified the rule in a matter-of-fact manner and reminded the student of the earlier mention of the rule. She also acknowledged her birthday and that it was a parent gift (versus ignoring it as in the original vignette).

3. When the teacher asked the student to take care of the problem, the student immediately sought permission for the game (which might be expected at this moment), the teacher shaped her response by telling her to get permission before recess and gave her some options for dealing with the game.

4. By following these steps, the teacher was able to address the problem, redirect the student to a reasonable solution, and assist the student to begin the class activity without confrontation or escalation.

## CHAPTER SUMMARY

Educators, parents, community members, and the student body for that matter, expect children to learn in a safe, orderly, productive, and nurturing environment. To accomplish these expectations, teachers need to have a number of rules, expectations, and procedures in place. To establish these working rules, teachers have to pay particular attention to teaching the rules and providing ongoing reminders and maintenance steps to ensure the practices are sustained over the course of the school year.

Once the rules are established, there will always be occurrences of situations where the students do not keep the rules or exhibit rule infractions. When students commit rule infractions in the classroom, it is most important that teachers employ strategies designed to defuse the situation and prevent ongoing engagement or class disruption and avoid escalation to further problem behavior.

A seven-step procedure was laid out in this chapter to defuse rule-infraction behavior along with examples involving K–12 students. The major emphases in these steps were to maintain the flow of instruction, carefully avoid power struggles with the students exhibiting the rule infractions, and—as far as possible—put the responsibility on the student to solve the problem. These goals can generally be accomplished by clarifying the rules, requesting the student to take care of the problem, and providing options as needed.

# PRACTICE EXAMPLE

The reader is invited to review the following classroom vignette and apply the same steps recommended in this chapter for addressing rule infractions.

## PRACTICE VIGNETTE

### Rule Infraction in Art Class

The art teacher, Ms. Rawinsky, has a routine where the students have to have all the materials on their table before they begin to draw. She has found this procedure is more efficient, there is less traffic during class, fewer accidents, and she can readily track what is needed. She reminds the students and explains this rule at the beginning of art class.

One student, Heather, collects an art sheet and begins to draw immediately, without getting the drawing materials.

The teacher works her way over to Heather and reminds her that she needs to get all of the materials for class before she starts to draw. Heather exclaims that she needs to draw first so that she doesn't spill any paint on her drawing. The teacher says quite clearly that Heather needs to stop drawing and get the rest of the materials. Heather continues drawing. The teacher then gives her a choice of getting the rest of the material, or she would have to go to the time-out area and read. Heather keeps drawing, ignoring the ultimatum. Ms. Rawinsky then sends her to the time-out area.

## Response Directions

1. Map the interaction pathway connecting the teacher–student interactions.

2. Identify the main teacher responses that may have contributed to the problem.

3. Identify the main student responses that may have maintained or worsened the situation.

4. Apply the steps for defusing this rule-infraction situation.

5. Note any additional comments.

**Note:** A response key for this problem is provided in Appendix J.

# 4

# *Defusing Disrespectful Behavior*

T eachers are well aware that providing instruction and assisting students to learn involves more than using a solid curriculum and employing sound instructional practices. Another crucial factor is the tone or quality of the classroom environment. If the classroom is calm, orderly, safe, and respectful, students will have more opportunity to focus on their instruction and learning. However, if the environment is chaotic, unsafe, and hostile relationships prevail in the classroom, the teaching–learning process will be significantly inhibited.

Schools have made a concerted effort over the past several years to establish schoolwide and classroom rules and expectations (Mayer, 2005; Sprague & Golly, 2004; Sugai & Horner, 2005). Typically, *respect for one another* is one of these standard behavioral expectations. Moreover, lack of respect or disrespectful behavior is commonly listed on office referral forms as a major school infraction (Spaulding et al., in press). Teachers have always viewed mutual respect, not only as desirable, but necessary for students to come to class, participate fully, and experience achievement at academic, social, and personal levels (Colvin, 2007; Scott, 2007; Sprick & Garrison, 2008).

Respect for one another in the classroom typically is addressed at two levels. The first level is respect between students. Typically, teachers have very systematic procedures for establishing respect between students, especially in the areas of respecting diversity, problem solving, and peer relationships. The second level, which is the focus of this chapter, involves respectful behavior between students and their teachers. In this chapter, details and procedures are described for teaching respect as a visible and functional priority in the classroom, and specific strategies for defusing disrespectful behavior are discussed.

## DESCRIPTION OF DISRESPECTFUL BEHAVIOR

*Respectful behavior* refers to the responses made by the students to other students or adults that are viewed as positive. Respect shows itself when students recognize the rights of others, especially in that every person in the school has a right to be there and to be treated with dignity and value. Respect is manifest by the way students treat others, talk to others, interact with others, talk about others, solve problems, and cooperate with others.

By contrast, *disrespect* refers to those behaviors from students that infringe upon the rights of others and are perceived as negative. Disrespectful behavior includes affronts directed toward others, such as insults, verbal assault, rudeness, put-downs, and slurs. Disrespectful behavior also includes bullying, harassment, intimidation, and hazing. These behaviors have quite harmful effects on the target persons or victims including embarrassment, fear, negative reactions, humiliation, anger, aggression, and withdrawal. Disrespect can significantly erode school climate and disrupt the teaching–learning process in the classroom. Disrespectful behavior from students toward teachers and school authorities can set the stage for antiauthoritarian behavior in students' adult life, leading to crime, dysfunctional relationships, and conflicts in the work place. Disrespect can be exhibited by words, gestures, written material, and body language. For example, a teacher may be explaining something important to a student, and the student grins and winks at another student. Clearly, disrespectful behavior is a serious disruptive behavior in schools and in classrooms and needs to be systematically and effectively addressed.

## PREREQUISITE CONDITIONS

Certain conditions need to be in place before the strategies presented in this chapter are implemented. Students are frequently exposed to examples of disrespect from the media, in the community, and in some cases, at home. Unfortunately, in some settings, disrespect toward others becomes the norm so that students from these settings do not see a problem when they exhibit disrespectful behavior at school, or when they see others engaging in the same behaviors. One student, for example, remarked in a school survey on harassment, "Racial jokes are okay if they are funny." In effect, this student has learned that the disrespectful behavior, racial jokes in this case, is acceptable under certain conditions.

Similarly, the school bully may be respected because he or she humiliates another student who is not liked. For these reasons, school districts, schools, and faculties need to take systematic steps to ensure that respect for one another becomes the norm among their students.

Prerequisite conditions are practices teachers and schools engage in to ensure that students clearly understand what respectful behavior is and why it is expected. The prerequisite conditions for respectful behavior are (1) systematically taught, (2) frequently and systematically acknowledged, and (3) regularly monitored and reviewed.

## Respectful Behavior Is Systematically Taught

School districts and schools are making a concerted effort throughout the nation to create a positive school environment for their students and faculty. Respect for one another needs to be one of the core values and is central to establishing the desired positive school environment. Just as cooperation with school rules and expectations need to be systematically taught and maintained (as discussed in Chapter 3), the same applies to the behaviors for respecting one another. Many exemplars exist in published literature and practices for teaching and maintaining schoolwide expectations, specifically respect for one another (Sprague & Golly, 2004; Sprick & Garrison, 2008; Sugai & Horner, 2005). The goal through this ongoing effort is to establish respect for one another as a *norm* in the school and district.

There are some additional topics that need to be addressed when respect is targeted on a schoolwide basis: (a) issues with diversity, (b) respect versus friendship, (c) teachers modeling respect, and (d) respect as a faculty norm.

### Issues With Diversity

Once schools address the expectation of respect for one another, they often find that students with singular characteristics, for example, ethnic and cultural distinctiveness or physical disabilities, often become targets for disrespect. In these cases, it is recommended that school personnel draw on the many published programs and literature that focus on these areas of concern such as *cultural and ethnic diversity* (Cooper, Chavira, & Mena, 2005; Henze, Norter, Sather, Walker, & Katz, 2002); *disabilities* (Cawley, Hayden, Cade, & Baker-Kroczynski, 2002; Scruggs & Mastropieri, 1996); and *bullying, harassment, and teasing* (Eisenberg, Neumark-Sztainer, & Story, 2003; Roberts, 2006).

### Respect Versus Friendship

Some students may become confused over the difference between respecting a student and liking and being friends with that student. Again, the solution lies in systematically teaching the students that respect is something due to *all* students, whereas friendship may be limited to *some* students. Or, respect is a right due to all students whereas friendship is a choice between students. In this regard, an elementary teacher has the classroom rule, "If you can't say something nice about someone, say nothing."

### Teachers Modeling Respect

One of the surest ways for teachers to lose respect of their students is to show disrespect to them. Students believe they have a right to be respected by their teachers, and when this does not occur, they are likely to reciprocate with disrespectful behavior and distance themselves from that teacher. By contrast, when teachers show respect to all their students, they not only model what respectful behavior looks like but they also establish effective relationships with their students.

### Respect as a Faculty Norm

Some teachers believe that respect is a school-community value and that if it is not practiced between faculty members, then there will be less carryover to students. Faculties also need to work at establishing and maintaining a professional working relationship between all its members.

## Frequently Acknowledge Students Who Display Respectful Behavior

Once respect for one another has been taught and established, the next prerequisite condition is for teachers to take steps to acknowledge students, in an ongoing manner, who display respectful behavior. When students regularly see that respectful behavior is reinforced by teachers, it becomes much easier to correct occurrences of disrespectful behavior.

Typically, teachers acknowledge students who cooperate with the classroom expectations at two levels. The first level is *informal*, where teachers catch students showing respectful behavior and acknowledge them directly, usually with praise. The second level is *formal*, where teachers have special recognition plans, such as awards, to acknowledge students for displays of caring and respect.

## PRACTICES ARE IN PLACE TO REGULARLY MONITOR AND REVIEW RESPECTFUL BEHAVIOR

Schools often undertake a project with high energy, but often as the year progresses, the energy gradually dissipates or is directed to other activities, resulting in a weakening of the initial project. Carefully monitoring the progress of school endeavors is essential to ensure the practices are sustained and goals achieved. One systematic measure for monitoring respectful behavior throughout a school is office-referral data. The forms used for office referrals usually list reasons for the referral, and respect is typically included on this list. In addition, other problem behaviors are directly related to respect, such as fighting, bullying, noncompliance, and defiance. By systematically reviewing office-referral data, school faculties can readily obtain information on the extent to which the behavior of respect for one another is operating within the school. With such data at hand, faculty can make decisions on action plans to address concerns if they arise.

Similarly, schools and classrooms often have recognition plans to acknowledge students who exhibit expected behaviors at an exemplary level. It is important to monitor whether these plans are sustained.

## CHECKLIST FOR PREREQUISITE CONDITIONS

Form 4.1, Prerequisite-Conditions Checklist and Action Plan for *Disrespectful Behavior* (Appendix E), is designed to assist teachers in determining if the prerequisite conditions identified in this section are adequately in place before the problem of disrespectful behavior is directly targeted.

## ILLUSTRATION FOR DISRESPECTFUL BEHAVIOR

In Box 4.1 (pages 67–68), a narrative description of the problem is provided with a corresponding depiction of an interaction pathway, analysis of teacher responses, and analysis of student responses. The analysis of teacher responses indentifies interactions that may have contributed to escalating the problem, taking considerable time to address, and making it likely that the same behavior will occur in the future. In the next section, recommended defusing steps for addressing disrespectful behavior are described, which will be applied to this illustration followed by a practice example at the end of the chapter.

## DEFUSING STEPS FOR ADDRESSING DISRESPECTFUL BEHAVIOR

There are six steps for addressing disrespectful behavior in the classroom: (1) assess the situation, (2) maintain the flow of instruction, (3) studiously avoid reacting to the disrespectful behavior, (4) pause and disengage, (5) address the student's behavior in a measured manner, and (6) debrief with the student at a later time.

**Form 4.1** Prerequisite-Conditions Checklist and Action Plan for *Disrespectful Behavior*

## Checklist for Disrespectful Behavior

*Scoring Key*

YES    The item is clearly in place

NO    The item is not in place, or there is uncertainty whether it is in place or not

### Items

YES  NO  1. Respectful behavior is taught as a schoolwide expectation

2. The following factors are addressed schoolwide as necessary

YES  NO  a. Issues with diversity

YES  NO  b. Clarification of respect versus friendship

YES  NO  c. Teachers model respectful behavior

YES  NO  d. Respect is the norm between faculty

YES  NO  3. Students are frequently acknowledged for showing respectful behavior

YES  NO  4. Practices are in place to regularly monitor and review respectful behavior practices

### Action Plan for Items Scored "NO"

_____

_____

_____

## BOX 4.1
## Disrespectful Behavior at Secondary Level

### Illustration

Angelo was wandering around the room, chatting to some students and reading the bulletin board during social studies. The teacher had already acknowledged the rest of the class for their productive engagement with the group activities. He then approached Angelo and said, in a calm and private manner, "Angelo, it really is time for you to be joining your group and getting on with the class work." Angelo quickly and loudly replied, "This class is boring, and you are boring too," while he stared at the teacher. The teacher moved closer to him and said, "I will not tolerate students talking to me like that." Angelo folded his arms and said, "So." The teacher then said, "So! My next step is to send you to the office for disrespect." Angelo retorted, "Send me wherever you like, and see if I care." He is then sent to the office for disrespectful behavior.

### Interaction Pathway

| Teacher Response | Student Response |
|---|---|
| Acknowledges class for engagement in class activity, approaches off-task student, and redirects him to join his group | |
| | Responds loudly that class is boring and so is the teacher |
| Moves closer to student and tells him that he will not tolerate talk like that | |
| | Folds his arms and says, "So" |
| Threatens to send student to office | |
| | Indicates he does not care about being sent to office (or anywhere) |
| Sends student to office for disrespect | |

**Analysis of Teacher Responses to Disrespectful Behavior**

- The teacher acknowledges the class for being on task productively.
- The teacher approaches the student who is off task and out of seat calmly and privately.
- The teacher redirects the student to the class activity (these first three responses were recommended in Chapter 2).
- The teacher reacts quickly to the student response "you are boring too" by moving closer to the student.
- The teacher takes the student response personally by stating such behavior will not be tolerated.
- The teacher reacts to the student's indifference ("So") with threat of office referral.
- The teacher sends the student to the office for his series of disrespectful behaviors.

**Analysis of Student Responses for Disrespectful Behavior**

- The student draws one-to-one attention from the teacher by being out of seat and off task.
- The student draws the teacher closer through a verbal response that the class is boring, and so is the teacher.
- The student obtains reaction from the teacher to the insult that he is boring too.
- The student draws a threat of office referral from the teacher by displaying indifference to teacher's response.
- The student is removed from class for displaying further indifference and disrespect for the remarks, "Send me anywhere . . ."
- The student is successful in being removed from the class and the class activity through successive disrespectful responses to the teacher.

### Step 1: Assess the Situation

Two questions must be addressed before the following defusing strategies are implemented. First, have the prerequisite conditions been met? The checklist and action plan, Form 4.1, Prerequisite-Conditions Checklist and Action Plan for *Disrespectful Behavior,* is designed to help answer this question and develop an intervention if needed.

The second question is, "How serious is the disrespectful behavior?" The behavior may involve serious disrespectful behavior, such as planned bullying or direct verbal abuse, involving expletives, toward a teacher. These behaviors typically warrant office referrals. In this book, the focus is on managing problem behavior that teachers are expected to address themselves versus the more severe behavior that warrants an office referral. This initial assessment is designed to determine whether the disrespectful behavior should be managed by teachers or referred to the office.

## Step 2: Maintain the Flow of Instruction

Per previous problem behavior addressed in Chapters 2 and 3, first and foremost, the teacher must make every effort to maintain the lesson or activity as if the disrespectful behavior had not occurred (again, presuming the behavior is one that the teacher is expected to manage). If the lesson stops or adjustments are *immediately* made, it is most likely that the student's problem behavior will be reinforced. For example, the teacher is explaining something to the class and notices a student talking and giggling. The teacher stops the explanation and approaches the student. By stopping the explanation and approaching the student in front of the whole class, the student may be highly reinforced by this level of attention. In addition, the behavior may escalate if the student needs to save face because the whole class is watching. Ideally, the teacher *must continue* with the explanation and not stop, pause, or stare at the student who may be trying to interrupt the class. The teacher conducts business as usual as the *first* response and *delays* responding to the interruption.

In addition, disrespectful behavior often arises when a teacher corrects or addresses an inappropriate behavior. For example, a student may be out of seat when the task is for students to be in their seats writing a report. The teacher provides a redirection to the student who then reacts with a disrespectful comment. In these cases, it is best to maintain the flow of instruction, particularly to acknowledge the students who are cooperating with the class activity and displaying the expected behaviors, as a *first* response. This action may correct the situation without the teacher needing to directly address the student's problem behavior or at least delay responding to this behavior. The order of responding conveys to the class that teacher attention first goes to the students who are cooperating with the lesson activity and classroom rules.

## Step 3: Studiously Avoid Reacting to the Disrespectful Behavior

Of the eight steps recommended for managing disrespect, this one is the *most important* and *most challenging* for teachers. When students exhibit disrespectful behavior toward their teachers, they are basically attacking their teachers in a personal manner. Consequently, it is difficult for teachers not to take the behavior *personally* and react. The teacher's reactive response then serves as a cue for the student's next response, often resulting in escalation and a more difficult situation.

The key principle is that the teacher's reaction *fuels* the student's next response and subsequent responses. In effect, the successive interactions are largely determined by the teacher's initial response to the student's display of disrespectful behavior.

Student's disrespectful behavior can often elicit angry or emotional responses from teachers, particularly when the student's behavior may be offensive, rude, or nasty. Angry responses from teachers can be manifested by shouting, getting in the student's face, finger pointing, threatening, glaring, rigidity in body language, and personal responses, such as, "How dare you talk to me like that?" or, "You listen to me. Don't you ever talk like that to me," accompanied with finger pointing. The problem is that angry responses like these are *highly likely to reinforce* the student's initial disrespectful behavior and *to set the stage* for further inappropriate behavior from the student, usually in the form of more confrontational behavior.

The core recommendation for managing disrespectful behavior from students directed at their teachers is to avoid reacting in ways that communicate anger, confrontation, or taking the behavior personally.

## Step 4: Pause and Disengage

It is one thing to recommend to teachers that they should not react and take the disrespectful behavior personally. However, it is more challenging to recommend what to do versus what not to do. When students exhibit disrespectful behavior, the strong recommendation is first to pause and second to disengage or delay responding.

The purpose of pausing, as a first response, is to lessen the chance of reinforcing the student's behavior. Disrespectful behavior is reinforced by quick and emotional responses. As one teacher put it, "They are jerking our chain, so we need to prevent that from happening." Or, as another teacher said, "They are trying to make us jump, and the first step is not to jump." The pause also gives the teacher a little time to control his or her own reactions so that a more measured response can occur.

The second, related part of this step is to disengage from the student. By disengaging, the student is getting the message that the teacher is not willing to engage with the student under these conditions. The simplest strategy for disengaging is to go to the other students. This step helps to maintain the flow of instruction and prevent other students from attending to the situation or participating in some way. Moreover, the student exhibiting the disrespectful behavior sees the teacher doing business as usual, which communicates to the student that, "Your disrespectful behavior is not affecting me."

Some teachers have reported that it is very difficult to disengage from a student under these conditions, and that by doing so, the student may be getting away with inappropriate behavior. This step is designed to break up an established interaction pathway where the student exhibits disrespect that is then followed by a reactive or direct response from the teacher, then the student responds with more inappropriate behavior, and so it goes, leading to a more-serious situation that is likely to be repeated. The intent of this pause-and-disengage step is to break up this pathway and establish a new, less-confrontational pathway that is more directed by the teacher.

## Step 5: Address the Student's Behavior in a Measured Manner

Once the teacher has disengaged from the student exhibiting the disrespectful behavior and made contact with the rest of the class (Step 4), the next step is to approach the student and address the disrespectful behavior. Four parts are recommended for this step: (1) use the student's name, (2) focus on the student's behavior, (3) deliver a consequence as appropriate, and (4) redirect to the class activity.

### Use the Student's Name

When the teacher returns to the student, after briefly connecting with the class, it is strongly recommended to begin the interaction by using the student's name. In doing so, the teacher not only secures the student's attention but also communicates respect to the student. It is well established that teachers use modeling as a primary tool for providing instruction and for teaching behavior. In this case, the teacher models respectful behavior by using the student's name in a context where the student has displayed disrespect to the teacher.

Moreover, when the teacher uses the student's name, there is less chance of the teacher showing anger or displaying body language that communicates an emotional reaction. Using the student's name helps to temper the behavior and language of the teacher.

### Focus on the Student's Behavior

After the teacher says the student's name, the next statement should be about what the student said—that is, to *name* the behavior. For example, "Monique, that kind of talk is very disrespectful." Similarly, "LeGarrett, that talk is hurtful." By naming the behavior as disrespectful, there is less chance of further confrontational engagement with the student compared to reacting to the behavior personally, saying something such as, "Don't you talk to me like that!"

### Deliver Consequence as Appropriate

It is usually appropriate for the teacher to deliver a negative consequence for disrespectful behavior. The purpose of the consequence is to communicate to the student that the disrespectful behavior was unacceptable and that it should not occur again. Typically, the teacher adds a consequence after the behavior has been named in the previous step. For example, "Monique, that kind of talk is very disrespectful; you will to take a time out." Or, "LeGarrett, that talk is hurtful. You will have to miss some recess. We can't have that talk."

Some teachers prefer to discuss the issue with the student at this moment to problem solve. This author recommends addressing these issues later, after the consequence has been delivered and the student is on track. The reason is that to problem solve, the teacher needs to be supportive and encouraging, which could reinforce the disrespectful behavior if conducted closely following the disrespectful behavior.

### Redirect to Class Activity

Once the consequence has been delivered, the teacher redirects the student to engage in the current activity. The directions should be presented in a clear and positive tone to communicate to the student that it is time to start over, and let's do it right this time. The teacher should also be ready to acknowledge the student briefly when he or she resumes the class activity.

## Step 6: Debrief With the Student at a Later Time

This contact with the student is usually conducted some time after the student is back on task. A common practice is for the teacher to say something like, "LeGarrett, I'd like to visit with you for a moment at the end of the class."

This visit is designed to encourage the student to solve the problem. If there is an agenda as to why the student uttered the disrespectful behavior, then the agenda can be addressed. Typically, teachers try to encourage students to find other ways to express their concerns or discontent. The author has developed a simple debriefing strategy based on three questions: What did you do? Why did you do it? and What else could you have done? (Colvin, 2004).

The teacher should also be ready to catch the student in subsequent situations where the student exhibits appropriate behavior versus the previous disrespectful behavior.

## CHECKLIST AND ACTION PLAN FOR DEFUSING DISRESPECTFUL BEHAVIOR

Form 4.2, Checklist and Action Plan for Defusing *Disrespectful Behavior* (Appendix F), is intended to be a resource for teachers so they can evaluate their responses to how disrespectful behaviors are managed in their classroom. The intent is for teachers to self-evaluate their responses to these problem behaviors, particularly to determine if they followed the recommended steps. For "yes" responses, the teacher is encouraged to maintain these responses consistently over time. Where "no" responses are recorded, the teacher is encouraged to develop an action plan to ensure the step is followed more reliably on the next occurrence of disrespectful behavior.

| Form 4.2 | Checklist and Action Plan for Defusing *Disrespectful Behavior* |
|---|---|

## Checklist for Defusing Disrespectful Behavior

**Steps**

1. A quick assessment made on occurrence of disrespectful behavior to determine

   a. Whether prerequisite conditions have been met    YES    NO
       If NO, prerequisite conditions need to be established

   b. Whether behavior warrants office referral    YES    NO
       If YES, follow with office referral
       If NO, defusing steps below followed

2. a. Flow of instruction maintained as a first response    YES    NO
   b. On-task students acknowledged    YES    NO

3. Studiously avoids reacting to disrespectful behavior    YES    NO

4. Pauses and disengages    YES    NO

5. Makes measured response to student's behavior

   a. Uses student's name    YES    NO
   b. Names student's behavior    YES    NO
   c. Delivers consequence    YES    NO
   d. Redirects student to class activity    YES    NO

6. Debriefs with student at later time    YES    NO

### Action Plan (for Any Items Scored "NO")

_____

_____

_____

# APPLICATION OF DEFUSING STEPS TO ILLUSTRATION OF DISRESPECTFUL BEHAVIOR

Earlier in this chapter, an illustration was described for a secondary class in which a student displayed disrespectful behavior (Box 4.1). The situation escalated, taking a considerable amount of teacher time, with a strong like-lihood that this kind of behavior would be repeated. The recommended steps for defusing disrespectful behavior are applied to this example in Box 4.2, followed by some comments.

## BOX 4.2
### Defusing Disrespectful Behavior Illustration for Secondary Level

### Recommended Defusing Steps for Managing Disrespectful Behavior

#### Step 1: Assess the Situation

The teacher concluded that the prerequisite conditions had been met (Form 4.1, Prerequisite-Conditions Checklist and Action Plan for *Disrespectful Behavior*). It was evident that the student had made a clear decision not to join the group or engage in the class activity. The teacher also concluded that the student's behavior was at a level that should be addressed within the classroom versus making an office referral or sending for assistance.

#### Step 2: Maintain the Flow of Instruction

The teacher had already acknowledged the class for being productively engaged in the group activity. He approached Angelo relatively slowly so that his attention could be given to students as he moved down the aisles toward Angelo. He simply looked at their work and paused to listen to some of their discussion, showing interest in their comments.

#### Step 3: Studiously Avoids Reacting to the Student Behavior

The teacher tried to redirect the student in a calm tone and a private, respectful manner, to which the student responded with the loud, disrespectful remark, "The class is boring, and you are boring too." The teacher realized that the remark was an insult or personal attack and was aware of the importance of not reacting and taking the remarks personally. He basically concluded that Angelo was having problems and was definitely not going to buy into his insult and confrontation.

#### Step 4: Pause and Disengage

Once the teacher held his own reaction in check, he looked at the student, looked at the class, and made an obvious response that he was pausing or deliberating. He then said to the student, "Just a second," and moved to the closest group of students, saw what they were up to, and made a positive comment about their efforts. He looked further around the room and said, "Looks like everyone is on track. Any questions?" He paused to see if there were any questions and then returned to Angelo.

#### Step 5: Address the Student's Behavior in a Measured Manner

The teacher now moves directly to Angelo, makes eye contact with him but does not crowd him, and says, "Angelo" (uses student's name). "What you just said is quite disrespectful" (names behavior and pauses). "I will need to take some action on that (pauses). You will have to miss the next break" (small negative consequence). The teacher then directs him to join the group, telling him that it will go better for him if he cooperates (redirection). If he joins the group, the teacher would acknowledge him briefly for cooperating. If he refuses to join the group or engages in further disrespectful behavior, the teacher would implement the recommended steps in Chapter 6 for defusing noncompliance and limit testing.

### Step 6: Debrief With the Student at a Later Time

The first-case vignette is that Angelo joined the group and participated in the class activity. After the teacher acknowledged him briefly for cooperating, he said, "I'd like to see you at the end of the period, please." When Angelo visited with the teacher, the teacher said, "Angelo, I want you to understand that your remarks were disrespectful. It was a personal attack on me. That is why you had to miss the break" (clarification of student's behavior and consequence). The teacher continued, "Now, was there something going on that I need to know or could help with?" (addressing possible reasons for the student being off task, leading to the disrespectful behavior). Based on the student's reply, the teacher might finish the visit with a comment like, "I sure hope you can get on with your work next time, and we do not have these problems. See what you can do."

The second-case vignette could be that the student maintained noncompliant behavior and ended up being sent to the office for noncompliance and disrespect. It is still recommended that the teacher would debrief with the student at the earliest opportunity and address the chain of events from refusing to participate in the class activity, the disrespectful remarks, and subsequent noncompliance. A useful strategy is the use the three questions, "What did you do?", "Why did you do it?", and "What else could you have done?" It is important for the exchange to end positively with encouragement from the teacher for the student to do better next time.

### Comments

1. The teacher worked hard to ensure that the rest of the students who were on task received his attention before any contact was made with the student off task.

2. The teacher had to make a concerted effort not to react to the insult from the student, was successful in controlling his reactions, and provided a delayed and measured response to the student. These steps increased the chances that the situation would be defused, and the student would begin to cooperate.

3. If the student did not cooperate, additional steps were available (steps for defusing noncompliance and limit testing in Chapter 6).

4. The debriefing session not only helps the student problem solve the situation, but it also helps to communicate to the student that there is closure on the issues.

## CHAPTER SUMMARY

Respect for one another is a cornerstone behavioral expectation for schools and classrooms. This expectation helps to set the stage for students to feel comfortable, with a strong sense of belonging, which is necessary for learning and achievement.

There are two aspects of respecting one another that educators need to systematically establish. The first concerns respect between students. This area includes teaching students to respect, honor, and celebrate diversity in its various forms. Moreover, systematic procedures are in place to address aberrations of respect such as teasing, bullying, harassment, hazing, and all forms of behavior where students target each other in disrespectful ways.

The second aspect of respect concerns behavior or interactions between students and their teachers. The major focus in the chapter was to describe procedures for defusing disrespectful behavior of students toward their teachers in the classroom. Prerequisite conditions were identified for classroom practices designed to establish respecting one another in the classroom. Steps were then described and illustrated for managing disrespectful behavior. One step is of paramount importance in the procedures: *to not take the disrespectful behavior personally.* Failure in this step can fuel further problems, while success can defuse the situation.

## PRACTICE EXAMPLE

The reader is invited to review the following classroom vignette and apply the same steps recommended in this chapter for addressing disrespectful behavior.

---

### PRACTICE VIGNETTE

#### Disrespect At Kindergarten Level

Ms. Sandursky, a kindergarten teacher, notices that two of her students are engaged in an argument over who should be playing with a particular toy during free time. She approaches the two students and says, "Rosalind and Tamara, listen to me, please. We need to share these toys." Rosalind interrupts the teacher, saying, "No. It's my turn," and makes a grab at the toy. The teacher takes the toy and tells Rosalind again that she needs to share. Rosalind shouts, "It's not fair. I hate you." The teacher, quickly takes her by the arm and says very firmly, "Listen. Don't you talk to me like that." Rosalind starts to scream and throws herself on the floor.

---

### Response Directions

1. Map the interaction pathway connecting the teacher–student interactions.
2. Identify the main teacher responses that may have contributed to the problem.
3. Identify the main student responses that maintained or worsened the problem.
4. Apply the steps for defusing this example of disrespectful behavior.
5. Note any additional comments.

**Note:** A response key for this problem is provided in Appendix K.

# 5

---

# *Defusing Agitation*

O ne of the most challenging behaviors teachers have to deal with in classrooms is acting-out behavior. Acting-out behavior can take many forms, such as running away, physical aggression, verbal abuse, serious confrontations and threats, sexual acting-out, vandalism, defiance and noncompliance, tantrums, and many different forms of anger outbursts. Teachers view this behavior as very serious because it can clearly disrupt the teaching and learning process for all students in the classroom, and it can pose a threat to safety for all persons in the classroom, the involved student, the teacher, and other students.

The author describes acting-out behavior as an escalated behavior pattern involving seven discrete phases: *calm, triggers, agitation, acceleration, peak, de-escalation,* and *recovery* (Colvin, 2004). The focus in this book is on defusing problem behavior. Consequently, for acting-out behavior to be defused, teachers must identify this escalated behavior pattern and *intervene early in the chain.* In this chapter, the target phase for defusing acting-out behavior is *agitation.* The logic is that if teachers are effective with managing the agitation phase, then subsequent, more-serious behaviors in the chain will be preempted. Serious student acting-out behavior is typically preceded by agitation. If this agitation period is managed successfully, the student will not proceed to exhibit serious acting-out behavior.

## DESCRIPTION OF AGITATED BEHAVIOR

*Agitation* is a general behavioral state that includes emotional dispositions, such as being angry, upset, depressed, on edge, withdrawn,

79

worried, disturbed, frustrated, or anxious. Teachers often describe these students as "being on edge," and usually it does not take much to tip them over the edge. In general, agitation can be manifest in one of two ways: (1) responses indicating *increases* in behavior and/or (2) responses indicating *decreases* in behavior. The following list provides examples of agitated behavior displayed by students as increases and decreases in behavior.

## Increases in Behavior

### Darting Eyes

Students look here and look there with a certain level of intensity but with little focus or purpose to their eye movements. Their eyes appear to fully engage, and then they shift to somewhere else.

### Busy Hands

Students often display a noticeable increase in hand movements, such as pencil tapping, drumming fingers, rubbing their thighs, opening and closing books, and tugging at their clothes. This behavior is very prevalent among students with severe disabilities, especially in the area of language and communication.

### Moving in and out of Groups

These students will want to join a group, and when they do, they want to join another group or do something else. They act as if they do not know what they want or as if nothing seems to engage their attention for very long.

### Off-Task and On-Task Cycle

Similarly, these students will start a task or activity and then stop and then start up again. There appears to be little, if any, fixed or sustained attention to academic tasks or classroom activities. They appear to be preoccupied.

### Easily Irritated by Other Students

Other students can quite easily irritate agitated students unintentionally just by looking at them, talking to them, talking to other students nearby, or making any kind of noise.

## Decreases in Behavior

### Staring Into Space

Students appear to be daydreaming and staring into space. They seem to be looking at something with a certain amount of concentration, but their minds are somewhere else. They may also appear to be "deaf" in that when things are said to them they do not give any indication that they have heard anything.

### Veiled Eyes

The students will avoid eye contact by looking away or looking down. Similarly, they will pull their hats down over their eyes or pull up the lapels of their jackets and sink their heads as low into their jackets as they can.

### Nonconversational Language

Student responses are such that it is difficult to build a conversation. For example, the teacher may greet the student and say, "Hi, Tony, how was your weekend?" The student then responds quite tersely, "Fine." The teacher then says, "What did you do?" Tony answers while looking away, "Nothing." Essentially the student is communicating that he does not wish to chat.

In some cases, the student's delivery is very subdued and difficult to hear. Again, the student is communicating that he or she does not want to engage in conversation.

### Contained Hands

By contrast to the group where busy hands were a signal of agitation, this group may hide their hands by sitting on them, folding their arms, or putting their hands behind their backs. Essentially, these students contain their hands as a strategy for disengaging from present academic tasks or classroom activities.

### Withdrawal From Groups

The students show a tendency to withdraw from the group, shut down, engage in independent activities, or move to isolated areas. There is the clear communication, "Leave me alone."

### Readily Attributes Blame

Agitated students are often very touchy, so they are quick to blame students for unintended events. For example, a student may walk by an agitated student and unintentionally bump him or her. The agitated student may blurt out, "You hit me on purpose."

## PREREQUISITE CONDITIONS

The procedures used to defuse agitation are designed to be a *short-term remedy*. That is, the teacher applies defusing techniques when a student may be exhibiting agitated behavior with the expectation that the student will settle down and participate in the class activity. However, if this student exhibits these same, or similar, agitated behaviors on a frequent basis, then more systematic supportive strategies need to be provided.

Recurring agitation is a clear sign that the student has needs that are not being met. In these cases, teachers or support personnel should conduct a functional behavioral assessment to determine the factors that may be contributing to and maintaining the student's agitation (Colvin, 2009; Carr & Wilder, 2004; Cipani & Schock, 2007; O'Neill et al., 1997). Once these factors have been identified, specific interventions can be designed and implemented to meet the needs of the student. The defusing strategies can still be used in conjunction with these systematic supportive interventions but not as stand-alone interventions.

## ILLUSTRATION FOR AGITATED BEHAVIOR

In the illustration from a specialist class, Box 5.1, a narrative description of a problem of agitated behavior is presented, and a corresponding depiction of an interaction pathway, analysis of teacher responses, and analysis of student responses follows. The analysis of teacher responses indentifies interactions that may have contributed to engaging the teacher over a lengthy period of time, escalating the situation, or making it likely the same or similar behaviors will occur in the future. In the next section, recommended defusing steps for addressing agitated behavior are described and applied to this illustration, followed by a practice example at the end of the chapter.

## DEFUSING STEPS FOR
## ADDRESSING AGITATED BEHAVIOR

Six steps are described for addressing agitated behavior in the classroom: (1) assess the situation, (2) maintain the flow of instruction, (3) identify the signs of agitation, (4) use calming strategies, (5) monitor accommodations, and (6) debrief with the student at a later time.

### Step 1: Assess the Situation

Two questions must be addressed before the following defusing strategies are implemented. First, how serious or intense is the agitated behavior? This determines whether the teacher should manage the problem or whether additional assistance is needed or whether an office referral should be made. For example, a student may have reached a state where he or she throws a chair across the room, pushes a desk over, and is threatening other students. Here, the teacher would determine that assistance is needed and follow school emergency procedures, as the behaviors are unsafe and very disruptive. Clearly, this student is upset, but the defusing strategies would not be appropriate in this context. The defusing strategies

## BOX 5.1
## Agitated-Behavior Illustration in Specialist Class, Computer Lab

### Illustration

Mr. Li, the computer lab teacher, was explaining to the class the goals and activities of the lesson during first period. Simone-Frances appeared at the door, hesitated, and entered the classroom, frowning as she walked, clutching her bag very tightly. As she approached her desk, she tripped slightly and dropped her bag. Some of the students sniggered. The teacher paused, telling her that she needs to sign the late form and to move quickly, as she was distracting the class. She muttered, "What do you think I am trying to do . . . (expletive)." The teacher asked her to sit at the side wall until she calmed down. Simone-Frances picked up her bag, turned around, and headed to the door shouting, "I'm out of here." The teacher asked the class to read the manual while he put a call into the office, relaying that a student had left the classroom without permission.

### Interaction Pathway

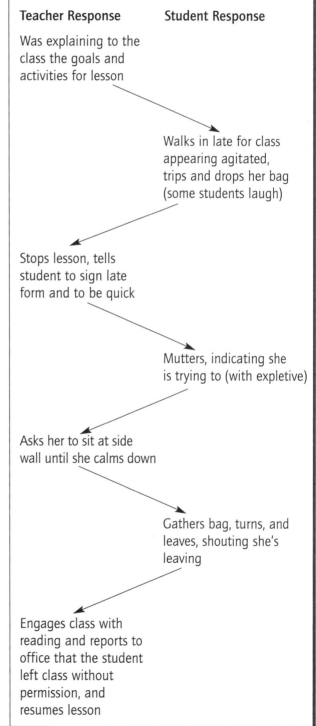

**Teacher Response**   **Student Response**

Was explaining to the class the goals and activities for lesson

Walks in late for class appearing agitated, trips and drops her bag (some students laugh)

Stops lesson, tells student to sign late form and to be quick

Mutters, indicating she is trying to (with expletive)

Asks her to sit at side wall until she calms down

Gathers bag, turns, and leaves, shouting she's leaving

Engages class with reading and reports to office that the student left class without permission, and resumes lesson

## Analysis of Teacher Responses to Agitated Behavior

- The teacher stops classroom activity when the student is late.
- The teacher draws attention to the student by stopping class and publicly telling her to sign the late form in front of the class.
- The teacher totally ignores the student's growing agitation and discomfort.
- The teacher delivers a reprimand (to hurry up and settle, as she is distracting the class) following a probable embarrassing moment when she dropped her bag and some students laughed.
- The teacher ignores the students who laughed when she dropped her bag.
- The teacher gives her a time out following a series of setbacks and probable embarrassments.
- The teacher follows the school procedure for students leaving class and resumes class (presumably as if nothing happened).
- Overall, the teacher ignored the escalating agitated behavior of the student and significantly contributed to her agitation by publicly addressing and reprimanding her. The teacher was more interested in following the procedures for students who come late to class and who leave class.

**Note:** The student, even though late for class, came to class. The "playing field is not level" when it comes to getting off to school in the morning. Some students receive adequate support at home in getting to school; others are basically left to their own resources, while some have to endure serious conflicts or problems in getting to school. Who knows what this student may have been dealing with to even get to school? Issues were evident by her initial level of agitation.

## Analysis of Student Responses for Agitated Behavior

- The student showed agitation as she entered the classroom. The student was probably dealing with some issues.
- The student tripped and dropped her bag, probably as a result of being embarrassed or annoyed by the teacher drawing attention to her for being late.
- The student muttered an expletive, showing further agitation, probably as a result of the students laughing and the teacher reprimanding her. To the student, it may have looked like the whole class was against her.
- The student reached a breaking point, walking out of class when the teacher gave her a time-out (sit at the side wall).
- Overall, the student showed increasing agitated behavior.
- The successive public interactions, corrections, and penalty along with students laughing escalated her behavior.

**Note:** It is highly likely that if this student is late in the future, she will not even show up for class as a result of the negative experiences on this occasion when she was late for computer lab.

are designed to address agitation in contexts that *do not pose a threat to safety and are minimally disruptive,* such as off-task behavior where the student may be mumbling, tapping a pencil, or sitting slouched in a chair.

The second consideration for this assessment is for the teacher to determine if the agitated behavior is a recurring concern. If the student is manifesting agitated behavior on a frequent basis, then more-systematic support needs to be made available for this student. Frequently occurring signs of agitation indicate that there are ongoing problems and triggers that need to be addressed for this student. In these cases, the student may need counseling, social-skills training, conflict-resolution training, parent involvement, or other intensive programs. The following defusing strategies are basically short-term interventions to be used for relatively infrequent occurrences of student agitation.

## Step 2: Maintain the Flow of Instruction

Per previous problem behaviors in earlier chapters, first and foremost the teacher must make every effort to maintain the lesson or activity. If the lesson stops, or adjustments are *immediately* made, it is most likely that the student's problem behavior may escalate to more-serious behavior. Typically when students are agitated, they want to be left alone. So when the teacher stops the lesson, additional attention is drawn to the student (not only from the teacher but from other students as well). Ideally, the teacher continues with the class activity and does not stop, pause, or immediately approach the student displaying agitation. The teacher conducts business as usual as the *first* response and *delays* responding to the student who is agitated.

## Step 3: Identify Signs of Agitation

Obviously, before the teacher can use defusing steps to reduce agitation, the teacher must be able to recognize the specific onset signs. Moreover, if the student displays agitation in other school settings, then it is possible for involved staff to obtain agreement on these signs of agitation for the student and implement the same, or similar, strategies to address the situation. In this way, the student experiences consistency across settings and is more likely to be successful throughout the school. Similarly, it may be appropriate to involve parents in the plan if the student displays similar agitated behavior at home. The parents would then recognize the signs of agitation and implement defusing steps to settle down their child and prevent further problems at home.

As noted early in this chapter (Description of Agitated Behavior), agitation can be manifest in one of two ways: (1) responses indicating *increases* in behavior; and/or (2) responses indicating *decreases* in behavior. Examples of increases or decreases in agitated behavior were described. The signs listed apply to students in general; however, there may also be specific signs an individual student manifests that are not included this list. These unique signs need to be noted and included in the following form under the heading *Other.* These general signs of agitation are listed at the end of this section, Form 5.1, Checklist and Action Plan for Defusing *Agitated Behavior* (Appendix G).

## Step 4: Use Calming Strategies

The central goal for managing agitation is to utilize strategies that enable the student to settle down, regain control, and participate in the class activity. The strategies are basically accommodations that are slight departures from the regular procedures. The assumption is that the regular procedures may escalate the student or at a minimum maintain the student's level of agitation. Because these strategies are supportive in nature, they must be implemented at the earliest *onset* of signs of agitation; otherwise, more serious behavior may be reinforced.

The following list of strategies for reducing agitation has been drawn from research and best practices (Ehrenreich & Fisak, 2005; Schoenfield & Morris, 2009; Sprick & Garrison, 2008). It is up to the teachers to find which strategies may be appropriate and effective for their students' age group and instructional setting.

### Teacher Empathy

Perhaps the most powerful supportive strategy a teacher may use is to convey *empathy*, which involves letting the student know that his or her agitation is recognized and that the teacher is concerned about it. For example, the teacher may see the student slouched in the chair staring at the floor (recognition) and then approaches the student and says, "Are you doing okay? Why don't you sit for a bit, and I'll be back shortly" (communicating concern). Empathy is usually more effective if the teacher has already established a good relationship with the student.

### Helping Student Focus on Class Activity

Agitated students typically have difficulty focusing on their work, getting started, staying on task, and concentrating. The reason is that they are essentially distracted by whatever it is that is disturbing them. The teacher can assist the students to get started with their work or continue if they have stopped working. For example, the teacher may help the student organize materials to get started or help them to clarify the lesson task.

### Providing Space

Students who are agitated generally want to be left alone. By permitting the student to have some space, or isolation, from the rest of the class helps to meet this need or validate the need. By being left alone, the student has the opportunity to gradually settle down and regain focus. For example, a teacher may permit the students to sit at their desks with their heads down for a while, go to another desk, or go to some designated area of the room.

### Present Options

When students are agitated, they are basically distracted. By presenting options to students, the teacher gives them a chance to focus and make a decision. This process helps students to take charge in a small way, which in turn helps them to calm down. For example, the teacher may approach a student who is agitated and ask her, "Abigail, would you like to sit here or down in the back where it is quieter?" Or, "Joe, how about getting the first five done, and you can do the rest later?"

### Providing Assurances and Additional Time

Students who are agitated often lack organization skills and the focus necessary to take charge of their responsibilities. Consequently, they may panic and exhibit worse behavior when certain tasks arise or responsibilities have to be met. In these situations, it is often helpful to give the student some *assurances,* and allow more *time* to deal with a task. For example, a teacher may say, "Take your time, Marcus, you have several minutes yet before the bell rings."

### Permit Preferred Activities

Students exhibiting agitation are usually absorbed with what is bothering them, making it difficult for them to concentrate on the classroom lesson or even to get started. Sometimes, a transition step is helpful, where the student is permitted to engage in a preferred activity for a limited time. This step helps students to disengage from what is bothering them and to focus on the preferred activity. It is then a small step to move to the lesson activity. For example, Charlie, a first-grade student, often has trouble on the bus, so when he enters the classroom he is already upset. The teacher has a designated desk in the corner of the room, so when Charlie enters he can immediately go to this spot and play with some Legos. Or Ana, an eighth-grade student who is frequently agitated when she comes to first period, is permitted to sit at the back of the room and read some magazines for a few minutes and then go to her desk.

### Teacher Proximity

Oftentimes when students become agitated, they become insecure, so standing near the student can provide a level of reassurance. Proximity strategies include standing near the student's desk when speaking to the class, making incidental contact with the student, and initiating brief interactions with the student, such as a comment or question, for example, "How is it going there, Bryan?" or "Looks like you have made a start there, Monika."

*Independent Activities*

In addition to serving several instructional purposes, independent work opportunities provide students with individual space. Independent work, by definition, helps to factor out interactions between students, providing a structure where the student is left alone. In effect, there are fewer distractions, giving the student more opportunity to focus on the instructional task. Independent work opportunities should be built into the regular classroom schedule and can be utilized when several students show signs of agitation.

*Passive Activities*

Following highly stimulating events, such as recess, gym, or assemblies, the whole class may be overly excited with several students in an agitated or excited state. Teachers may effectively use passive strategies to calm down the class. These activities require attention from the students but not much in the way of effort to respond, such as watching a short video, silent reading, or listening to the teacher read.

*Movement Activities*

Movement is a tool that teachers can use to help a student who is agitated. Many students automatically show an increase in movement when they are agitated. Consequently, when the teacher provides students with an opportunity to move, there is more chance that the students' needs will be met, helping them to become calm and focused. Strategies involving movement include distributing materials for class, running an errand, or putting materials away.

*Student Self-Management*

Self-management is the ultimate, long-term goal of any intervention program for problem behavior. Consequently, it is very important to actively involve students, where appropriate, in a plan to control agitation. Students often have their own strategies to reduce agitation and can contribute to the plan or program. For example, Micah had the practice of running away from the classroom when he became upset. So, the teacher arranged with him that instead of running away from the school, he was permitted to go to a designated desk in the library. After some time of success with this strategy, the teacher was able to adapt the plan for him to go to a designated quiet place in the classroom. Essentially, the student needed a place to go when he became upset and was given the opportunity to go to these designated areas when he recognized his own agitation.

## Step 5: Monitor Accommodations

It is very important for teachers to monitor the application of these defusing strategies for managing agitation in the classroom for two reasons.

First, as the strategies are basically accommodations where students are provided with supportive measures to help them calm down and participate in the class activities, some students may realize that they can get out of their work by "being agitated." That is, they may conclude, "I don't feel like doing math right now. I am agitated." This situation can be addressed when the plan is set up initially. The teacher needs to tell the student that these strategies will be used just for a while at no cost. However, after a short time, when the student is doing better, the student will be required to make up the time or catch up on the task that is missed.

The second reason for monitoring occurrences of agitation where the strategies are employed relates to the issue of persistent states of agitation. If the monitoring data show that the student is frequently agitated, even though the defusing strategies help to calm the student down, additional interventions are needed. Frequent occurrences of agitation indicate that there are triggers or causes that need to be identified and directly addressed in a more-comprehensive plan.

### Step 6: Debrief With the Student at a Later Time

This contact, as with defusing strategies in earlier chapters, is usually conducted some time after the student is back on task. A common practice is for the teacher to say something like, "LeGarrett, I'd like to visit with you for a moment at the end of the class."

This visit is designed to encourage students to review the process of how the accommodation worked for them. If the procedure was successful, the student would be acknowledged for settling down and getting back on task. If there were additional concerns, these could be addressed and alternative defusing strategies could be identified for future occasions.

In addition, the teacher would prompt students to examine why they were agitated in the first place and then help them solve the problem. Teachers could also use this opportunity to discuss with the student a plan for phasing out the defusing accommodation as the student becomes more successful.

### Other

The above list of defusing strategies is not meant to be exhaustive. It is very likely that the teacher may effectively use additional strategies to defuse agitated behavior. These strategies should be noted.

## CHECKLIST AND ACTION PLAN FOR DEFUSING AGITATED BEHAVIOR

Form 5.1, Checklist and Action Plan for Defusing *Agitated Behavior* (Appendix G), is intended to be a resource for teachers, so they can evaluate their responses to how agitated behaviors are managed in the classroom. The intent is for teachers to self-evaluate their responses to these behaviors, particularly to determine if they followed the recommended steps. For "yes" responses, the teacher is encouraged to maintain these responses consistently over time. Where "no" responses are recorded, the teacher is encouraged to develop an action plan to ensure the step is followed more reliably on the next occurrence of agitated behavior.

**Form 5.1**    Checklist and Action Plan for Defusing *Agitated Behavior*

## Checklist for Defusing Agitated Behavior

**Steps**

1. A quick assessment made on occurrence of agitated behavior to determine

   a. Whether behavior should be managed by teacher or office          YES    NO

   b. Whether behavior is frequent, warranting more-intensive intervention          YES    NO

   If YES, initiate more intensive plan

   If NO, defusing steps below followed

2. a. Flow of instruction maintained as a first response          YES    NO

   b. On-task students acknowledged          YES    NO

3. Signs of agitation identified          YES    NO

*Increases in Behavior*

- ❏ Darting eyes
- ❏ Busy hands
- ❏ Moving in and out of groups
- ❏ Off-task and on-task cycle
- ❏ Easily irritated by other students
- ❏ Other

*Decreases in Behavior*

- ❏ Staring into space
- ❏ Veiled eyes
- ❏ Nonconversational language
- ❏ Contained hands
- ❏ Withdrawal
- ❏ Readily attributes blame
- ❏ Other

4. Use calming strategies                                              YES        NO
   ❏ Teacher empathy
   ❏ Helping student focus on class activity
   ❏ Providing space
   ❏ Present options
   ❏ Providing assurances and additional time
   ❏ Permit preferred activities
   ❏ Teacher proximity
   ❏ Independent activities
   ❏ Passive activities
   ❏ Movement activities
   ❏ Student self-management
   ❏ Other

5. Monitor accommodations                                              YES        NO

6. Debrief with student at later time                                  YES        NO

**Action Plan (for Any Items Scored "NO")**

_____

_____

_____

_____

_____

_____

# APPLICATION OF DEFUSING STEPS TO ILLUSTRATION FOR AGITATED BEHAVIOR

Earlier in this chapter, an illustration was described for a specialist class, computer lab, in which a student displayed agitated behavior (Box 5.1). The situation escalated, taking a considerable amount of teacher time, and there was a strong likelihood that this kind of behavior would be repeated. The recommended steps for defusing agitated behavior will now be applied to this example, Box 5.2, followed by some comments.

## BOX 5.2
## Defusing Agitated Behavior for Specialist Class, Computer Lab

### Recommended Defusing Steps for Managing Agitated Behavior

### Step 1: Assess the Situation

The teacher, Mr. Li, was not aware that Simone-Frances had any previous problems. He was also comfortable in thinking that her behavior was at a level he should take care of in the classroom.

### Step 2: Maintain the Flow of Instruction

Mr. Li noticed Simone-Frances appear at the door after class had started. However, he made no immediate response to her, and continued with his explanation for today's lab work. Meanwhile, Simone-Frances moved to her seat. Mr. Li approached Simone-Frances when the students were engaged in setting up for the class work. By waiting until the class was engaged, Mr. Li was able to approach Simone-Frances more privately, and this also gave Simone-Frances some time to get settled.

### Step 3: Identify Signs of Agitation

Mr. Li could see immediately that Simone-Frances was upset over something by the way she was frowning, walking while clutching her bag, tripping, and dropping her bag.

### Step 4: Use Calming Activities

Mr. Li was concerned that even though Simone-Frances was late for class, she was obviously upset and he was not pleased with the students laughing when she tripped and dropped her bag. Without changing pace at all with his explanation, he moved toward Simone-Frances, helped her pick up her bag, and completed his explanation (*teacher support and empathy*). Once the class was engaged in the beginning activities he approached Simone-Frances as privately as possible saying, "Glad you made it to class, let's get the materials set up, and I'd appreciate it if you would fill out the form for the office" (*teacher proximity; helping student focus on class activity*). When the form was completed, Mr. Li asked Simone-Frances to distribute a worksheet to each student (*movement activity*).

Mr. Li also approached the group of students who laughed when she tripped and dropped her bag and said in a quiet manner, "Listen, please. I noticed some of you laughing when a student came in late and dropped her bag. Please don't do that. It is embarrassing for the student and not very classy. Okay?" He then made an announcement about how pleased he was with everyone's work in class today.

### Step 5: Monitor Accommodations

Mr. Li decided to keep an eye on Simone-Frances over the next few classes to watch for further signs of agitation. He was well aware that he gave Simone-Frances more attention and assistance than normal. He monitored her throughout the class, noting that she was on task and productive.

### Step 6: Debrief With the Student at a Later Time

Mr. Li asked Simone-Frances to see him at the end of class. During this visit, he commented on how pleased he was with her getting on track with the class even though she had a rough start. He also mentioned that he saw that she was upset coming into class and said that if there is anything he could help with to let him know.

### Comments

1. The teacher ensured that Simone-Frances received as little attention as possible when she entered, to minimize embarrassment.

2. He helped her with her bag, showing support to her as well as to the rest of the class, and he kept his explanations going without a pause.

3. The teacher acknowledged the student for coming to class even though she was late. He was aware that several students in the school had attendance issues, and he preferred her to come in late versus not coming in at all. She also may have a legitimate reason for being late and should not experience negative consequences.

4. He briefly and directly addressed the students who had added to her embarrassment by laughing at her.

5. The teacher also followed, in a discreet and nonconfrontational manner, the protocol of filling out a form for being later for class.

6. Overall, the teacher was supportive and empathetic in managing his student's agitation, settling her down, and avoiding further escalation.

## CHAPTER SUMMARY

Students display agitated behavior on a relatively frequent basis in the classroom, as there are many causes for students to become upset in school settings. It is very important for teachers to effectively manage agitated behavior among their students for two reasons. First, students who are agitated can easily become more upset and display escalated or more-serious behavior. Second, when students are agitated they may shut down or become quite distracted, making it very difficult for them to participate effectively in instruction.

One of the challenges facing teachers in managing their students' agitated behavior in the classroom is to recognize the signs. Typically, teachers are engaged with instruction involving several students. In this context, it is sometimes difficult to recognize the signs or behaviors indicating that one or more of the students are upset over something. Moreover, it is most important to catch the signs of agitation as early as possible before the student has the opportunity to become more upset and exhibit more-serious behavior.

There are many strategies teachers can use in a classroom to help a student calm down and become engaged in the class activities. The most important first step in using these strategies is *teacher empathy*, where the teacher communicates to the students that their agitation is recognized, that the teacher is concerned about it, and is willing to make some accommodations to help them to settle down.

Teachers must be careful to monitor their use of calming strategies; otherwise, some students may abuse or exploit the accommodations made available to them. In addition, some students may have some serious ongoing issues causing their agitation. The calming strategies described in this chapter are meant to be short-term interventions to help settle a student down in the classroom. These defusing strategies do not target the causes or triggers that may have caused the agitation in the first place. In these cases, more assessment will be needed, leading to more-systematic and comprehensive intervention plans.

## PRACTICE EXAMPLE

The reader is invited to review the following classroom vignette and apply the same steps recommended in this chapter for addressing agitated behavior.

### PRACTICE VIGNETTE

#### Agitated Behavior in Secondary

During independent work in math, students are expected to complete problems that were assigned in the previous class. One student, Roland, is sitting slouched in his seat, feet stretched out, head down, staring at the floor, and looking very serious. The teacher, Ms. Hendley, approaches him saying, "Roland, it is time to get started on your math." Roland, without raising his head, says loudly, "I'm done." The teacher looks over Roland's shoulder and sees that he completed some of the problems, but not all. The teacher says, "Roland, you have made a good start, but please get on with it and finish up the assignment." Roland rounds his shoulders, puts his head down, and says, "I am not doing this stuff twice." The teacher says, "If you need help let me know, otherwise if you don't finish it, your grades will be down." Roland says, "Pshaw..." and waves his arm to dismiss the teacher. The teacher moves away to another student.

### Response Directions

1. Map the interaction pathway connecting the teacher–student interactions.

2. Identify the main teacher responses that may have contributed to the problem.

3. Identify the main student responses that maintained or worsened the problem.

4. Apply the steps recommended for defusing agitated behavior.

5. Note any additional comments.

**Note:** A response key for this problem is provided in Appendix L.

# 6

# *Defusing Noncompliance and Limit Testing*

Noncompliance, limit testing, defiance, and all of those behaviors related to students' *refusal to cooperate* with their teachers, are considered to be particularly challenging and very detrimental to the teaching-learning process in the classroom (Colvin, 2009; Cotton, 2000; Lane, Wehby, & Cooley, 2006; Sprick & Garrison, 2008). For example, if the teacher needs to explain the math assignment on page 54, how can instruction proceed if some students refuse to open their books to page 54 or attend to the teacher's explanations? Moreover, noncompliance, especially defiance, has an element of confrontation in it, so that when the teacher addresses the behavior, the student may become more confrontational and belligerent, leading to serious escalation and disruption.

Several researchers have reported that noncompliance, defiance, insubordination, and variations of lack of cooperation in class have been one of the most, if not the most, common reason for office referrals from classrooms across all grade levels (May et al., 2003; Skiba, Peterson, & Williams, 1997; Spaulding et al., in press). These data suggest that teachers, in general, have a difficult time managing noncompliant behavior in the classroom.

The purpose of this chapter is to address noncompliance and limit testing from the specific angle of interactions between the teacher and students. There is no assumption that this focus will ameliorate all problems in this area. But, there is sufficient basis to say that if these interactions are properly understood and teachers use effective defusing strategies, the problems will be lessened.

## DESCRIPTION OF NONCOMPLIANCE AND LIMIT TESTING

Noncompliance and limit testing have various names or synonyms in schools depending on the area, school culture, and the student age group. Some of these synonyms include oppositional behavior, insubordination, defiance, refusal to follow directions, resistance to directions, noncooperative behavior, willfulness, stubbornness, not minding, and nonconforming.

Essentially, *noncompliance* refers to those student behaviors where a teacher makes a request, and the students do not fulfill the request satisfactorily. For example, the teacher asks the students to sit down and begin their work. Most of the students follow the direction, sit down, and begin their work (*compliance or cooperation*), while some students remain out of their seat and do not follow the direction (*noncompliance*).

Noncompliance can be manifested in a variety of ways from overt refusal, as in defiance, to more subtle forms of resistance where students follow the direction in a marginal manner, such as limit testing. For example, a teacher asks one student to join the group, and the student glares at the teacher and says, "Make me" (*defiance*). Or, a student is asked to join the group and instead fiddles with items on the bulletin board, walks across the room, talks to someone, and then joins the group. This student follows the direction but takes an unreasonable amount of time in doing so (*limit testing*).

For the purposes of this book, *noncompliance* refers to those behaviors displayed by students where it is quite clear that they are not going to follow the teacher's directions or requests. *Limit testing*, a form of noncompliance, and a very common problem behavior in the classroom, includes behaviors where there is partial compliance. That is, the student fulfills the teacher's request to an *unsatisfactory standard*. These students, as some teachers say, "See what they can get away with." While noncompliance and limit testing are somewhat different in operation, the same defusing strategies are recommended for both types of behavior.

## PREREQUISITE CONDITIONS

The defusing strategies presented in this chapter for addressing noncompliance and limit testing are based on the assumption that the teacher is reasonably certain that the student's behavior is clearly noncompliant. Before student behavior can be labeled noncompliant, certain conditions must be met. If these conditions are not met, the behavior should not be called noncompliance. This does not mean that the behavior is not a problem. Rather, it means that defusing strategies for addressing noncompliant behavior may not be appropriate for addressing this behavior. Conversely, if the following conditions are in place, the teacher may apply the defusing strategies with a reasonable expectation of success.

## School Authority

In order for a student to exhibit noncompliant behavior, a direction must be given by an authorized *school authority*. A *person in authority* refers to any member of the faculty, which includes administrators, certified and classified staff, substitute teachers, and in some cases, approved volunteers.

## Following Directions Taught as Classroom Expectation

Cooperation, specifically following teacher directions, must be taught and established as a classroom expectation. Teachers should use strategies to frequently acknowledge students who cooperate so that following directions becomes the norm in the classroom.

Classroom directions may be *explicit* or *implicit*. An explicit direction is unambiguous in its interpretation and is directly delivered. For example, the teacher may present a direction to the class, "Open your math book to page 54, please." There is no question as to what book and page is needed and what the students are expected to do.

Other directions are implicit. These usually include established routines, expectations, and rules in the classroom. For example, the teacher may say, "Listen, everyone, it is time for music." The directions implied in this announcement are for the students to follow the routine of putting their materials away, clearing their desks, pushing in their chairs, and lining up at the door. It is assumed that implicit directions have been taught and established so that the students and staff know exactly what is required.

## Understanding the Directions

It is particularly important to ensure that the students clearly understand the directions and know what is required of them. Obviously, student responses to directions cannot be assessed as compliant or noncompliant if the students did not properly understand the directions. Moreover, the language used in the directions needs to be age appropriate and specific enough that the tasks required of the students are clear.

## Ability to Fulfill Directions

The student must have the necessary skills to complete the task before a judgment can be made on whether or not the student is being noncompliant. If the student does not have the skills to complete the task, then further instructional assistance is needed. If the student can complete the task but will not, then there is a basis for assessing the behavior as noncompliant.

## Positive Delivery

In some cases, students may react and exhibit noncompliance because of the teacher's tone or body language when the direction is delivered. The analysis of the student behavior is not so much a compliance issue; rather, it is a negative or retaliatory response to the teacher. Teachers should present directions to the students in a calm and respectful manner.

### Securing Student Attention

Teachers must secure the students' attention prior to delivering a direction. If the students are attending to something else, it will be difficult for them to attend to the direction. In these situations, teachers need to disengage the students from what they are currently attending to and then present the direction.

Form 6.1, Prerequisite-Conditions Checklist and Action Plan for *Noncompliance and Limit Testing* (Appendix H), is designed to assist teachers to determine if the prerequisite conditions are adequately in place before any problem behavior is directly targeted as noncompliance or limit testing.

In the first part of the form, the responses to each item are simply "yes" or "no." If there is doubt for any item, or if the response is unknown, the item should be recorded as a "no" and addressed in the action plan. The second part of the form is the action plan where the teacher identifies steps to be taken to address any item that is recorded as a "no" in the checklist.

---

**Form 6.1**    Prerequisite-Conditions Checklist and Action Plan for *Noncompliance and Limit Testing*

---

### Checklist for Noncompliance and Limit Testing

*Scoring Key*

| | | |
|---|---|---|
| YES | NO | 1. Direction delivered by school authority |
| YES | NO | 2. Following directions taught as classroom expectation |
| YES | NO | 3. Directions are understood |
| YES | NO | 4. Students have ability to fulfill directions |
| YES | NO | 5. Directions delivered positively |
| YES | NO | 6. Students' attention secured |

#### Action Plan (for Any Items Scored "NO")

_____

_____

_____

# ILLUSTRATION FOR NONCOMPLIANCE AND LIMIT TESTING

In the illustration of noncompliant and limit testing behavior from a secondary class, Box 6.1, a narrative description of the problem behavior is presented along with a corresponding depiction of an interaction pathway, analysis of teacher responses, and analysis of student responses. The analysis of teacher responses indentifies interactions that may have contributed to escalating the situation, taking additional teacher time, or making it more likely that the same problems will occur in the future. In the next section, recommended defusing steps for addressing noncompliant and limit-testing behavior are described, which will be applied to this illustration, followed by a practice example at the end of the chapter.

# DEFUSING STEPS FOR ADDRESSING NONCOMPLIANT AND LIMIT-TESTING BEHAVIOR

There are six steps for addressing noncompliance and limit testing in the classroom: (1) assess the situation, (2) maintain the flow of instruction, (3) repeat direction privately, (4) disengage and respond to the class, (5) provide focus on student decision making, and (6) debrief with the student at a later time.

## Step 1: Assess the Situation

Two questions must be addressed before the following defusing strategies are implemented. First, how serious or intense is the noncompliance or limit testing? The response determines whether the teacher should manage the problem or an office referral should be made. For example, a student may be refusing to follow directions and at the same time shouting and throwing things around the room. Here, the teacher would determine that an office referral should be made, or school emergency procedures followed as the behaviors are unsafe and very disruptive. In another example, a student may refuse to follow directions and just sit in his desk without displaying any level of disruption. The teacher would normally address this situation in the classroom. The defusing strategies are designed to address noncompliance and limit testing in contexts that *do not pose a threat to safety and are minimally disruptive.*

The second consideration for this assessment is whether the prerequisite conditions have been met. The checklist and action plan in Form 6.1, Prerequisite-Conditions Checklist and Action Plan for *Noncompliance and Limit Testing*, is designed to help answer this question and develop an intervention if needed.

## BOX 6.1
## Noncompliance and Limit Testing Illustration at Secondary Level

| Illustration | Interaction Pathway |
|---|---|

The ninth-grade history class was writing a one-page summary on the purchase of the Louisiana Territory. The class was well under way while one student, Anne-Louise, was sitting with her arms folded. The teacher, Mr. Pavretti, was moving around the room, checking students' work and answering questions. As he came to Anne-Louise's desk he saw she had written two lines. So, he said, "Anne-Louise. Need any help?" She said, "No. I am done." The teacher said, "Well, I am glad you've started, but the assignment is to write a full-page report." Anne-Louise replied, "I've said it all, and that's it." The teacher said, "Well, I fail to see how you can be done with only two lines when there are many steps in the process. Look, I can help you, or you can read some more, but you need to do a full-page report." Anne-Louise crossed her arms, stared at the teacher, and said, "I'm not doing any more. Why waste my time on this? It's boring." The teacher said, "Well, boring or not, that is the assignment, and there is no way you can get a passing grade with just two lines." He then walked away, going to other students while Anne-Louise remained seated

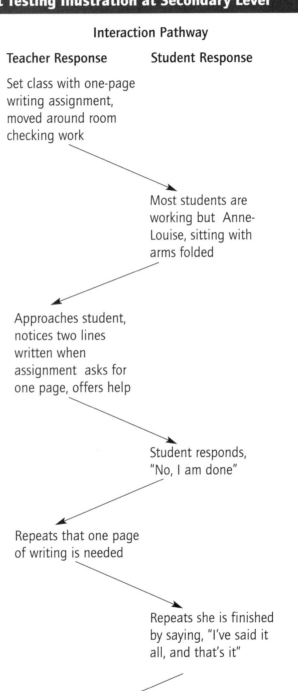

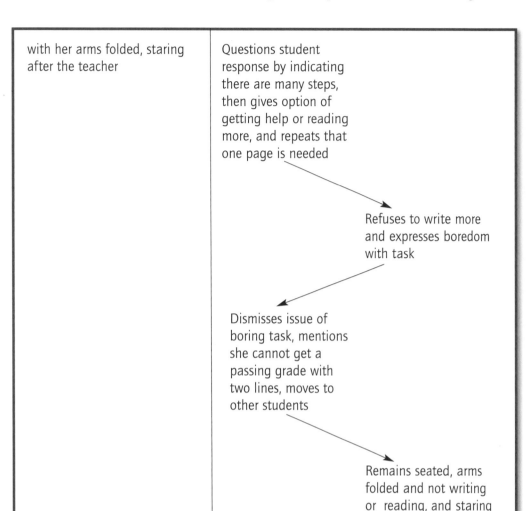

with her arms folded, staring after the teacher

Questions student response by indicating there are many steps, then gives option of getting help or reading more, and repeats that one page is needed

Refuses to write more and expresses boredom with task

Dismisses issue of boring task, mentions she cannot get a passing grade with two lines, moves to other students

Remains seated, arms folded and not writing or reading, and staring after the teacher

**Analysis of Teacher Responses to the Noncompliance and Limit Testing**

- The teacher moves around class checking student work, responding to questions as needed (normal good-practice routine).
- The teacher notices Anne-Louise has stopped working and has written two lines, when the assignment requires a full page.
- The teacher offers help and clarifies the task assignment.
- The teacher responds somewhat to student's defiance statement of, "I've said it all, and that's it," by saying, "Well, I fail to see . . . ," that is, the teacher engages with the student.
- Following further resistance, the teacher brings up the consequence of not being able to get a passing grade with just the two lines of work.
- The teacher moves to other students.
- Overall, the teacher became engaged with the student and then had to disengage by walking away.

---

**Analysis of Student Responses for Noncompliance and Limit Testing**

- The student caught teacher's attention by not working and having only two lines of a one-page assignment completed.
- The student sustained resistance to help, avoidance of task, and engaged the teacher.
- The student was successful in engaging the teacher in an argument or discussion on the task by displaying noncompliance and in not completing the request or task satisfactorily.

---

## Step 2: Maintain the Flow of Instruction

Per problem behaviors in earlier chapters, first and foremost, the teacher must make every effort to focus on the lesson activity and especially on the students who are cooperating. If the lesson stops, or the student displaying noncompliant behavior is addressed immediately, this student's noncompliant behavior is likely to be reinforced. In addition, the students who are cooperating learn that the teacher provides attention to noncompliant behavior first and to cooperative behavior second. The model throughout this book is that the teacher conducts business as usual as the *first* response, which includes acknowledging the students for cooperation first and *delays* responding to the noncompliant behavior.

## Step 3: Repeat Direction Privately

There is always the possibility that the student who is not following the direction may not have heard the request or understood it. Once the lesson or activity is under way, and the class is engaged, the teacher could then approach the student directly and privately. This step enables the teacher to secure the student's attention fully and ensure that the student does not have an audience as the rest of the class is engaged with the lesson activity. The teacher simply repeats the direction and provides the student with an opportunity for questions in case further clarification is needed. The teacher would then move to the rest of the class.

## Step 4: Disengage, Respond to the Class, and Monitor

Once the teacher has repeated or clarified the direction, it is most important for the teacher to withdraw and go to the other students. In contrast, if the teacher stays with the student waiting to see a cooperative response, a power struggle may ensue, and the student will focus more on the teacher than on the teacher's request. By withdrawing, the teacher provides the student with a little space to decide whether to follow the direction or not.

The teacher has given this student additional attention for not following directions, so it is important to give attention to the other students who are cooperating with the directions and class activity. While the teacher is moving around or directing attention to the rest of the class, the student who was noncompliant initially needs to be monitored. All this would involve is a glance or two toward the student to see whether or not the direction has been followed. If the student follows the direction, the teacher would acknowledge the cooperation briefly. If the student did not follow the direction, the teacher would proceed to Step 5.

## Step 5: Provide Focus on Student Decision Making

The overall focus on this step is to put the responsibility for following directions clearly with the student. In many cases, the noncompliance is designed to challenge the teacher, setting the stage for a power struggle. Whether the student is successful in creating a power struggle depends on how the teacher responds. This step is a planned procedure from the teacher to minimize the chance of engaging in a power struggle and help students focus on what is being requested in the lesson. There are four parts to this procedure: (1) establish initial setup, (2) use a nonconfrontational delivery, (3) present the request as a decision, and (4) follow through based on student decision.

### Establish Initial Setup

When noncompliant situations arise, the teacher should explain beforehand how these situations will be managed so that there are no surprises for the students. Moreover, teachers don't have to rack their brains as to how they will respond "in the heat of the moment." Teachers typically review their management procedures with their classes at the beginning of the year. These steps would be included in this review. In addition, teachers should have at their fingertips a short list of negative consequences that they can use when needed, such as time-out, loss of points, loss of a privilege, detention, or an office referral, depending on the gravity of the situation.

### Use a Nonconfrontational Delivery

The way in which the teacher approaches the student—body language, words used, and tone—is critical for preventing a power struggle. The teacher needs to maintain *calmness and respect* in approaching the student and avoid behaviors likely to escalate the student's behavior (such as shouting, agitation, threatening, finger pointing, and crowding the student). A business-like and matter-of-fact tone of voice is recommended.

*Present the Request as a Decision*

The teacher does three things:

1. Informs the students that a decision has to be made: follow the request as asked or face a negative consequence;

2. Allows some time for the student to decide (usually less than a minute); and

3. Withdraws from the student and attends to the other students in the class.

For example, Mickaleb is not following a direction and has had the direction clarified (Step 4). His teacher approaches him calmly and says in a matter-of-fact manner, "Mickaleb, you have been asked to get started on your math" (*expected behavior/request*), "or you will have to do it during the break" (*negative consequence*). "You have a few seconds to decide" (*time to decide*). The teacher then moves to other students (*withdraws*).

*Follow Through Based on the Student's Decision*

The teacher returns to the student to determine whether or not the student has followed the request. There are typically three possibilities:

1. The student has followed the request satisfactorily. In this case, the teacher acknowledges the decision briefly and continues with the lesson. Note, it is important to acknowledge the choice briefly, as some students may react negatively given they did not get their own way.

2. If the student does not follow the request satisfactorily but instead maintains the noncompliant behavior, the teacher follows through and delivers the negative consequence.

3. Once students become familiar with the teacher's follow-through procedure, it is common for them to try a delayed manipulation tactic (limit testing). They will maintain the problem behavior, and after they are told that the negative consequence will be delivered, they switch and follow the expected behavior. In these cases, the teacher needs to *follow through* with the negative consequence in order to establish limits. It might be reasonable to modify the consequence to some extent, for example, have the student miss part of recess on the basis that the student did eventually begin work. It is important to review this response during the debriefing step (Step 6).

### Step 6: Debrief With the Student at a Later Time

This contact, as with defusing strategies in earlier chapters, is usually conducted some time after the student is back on task and the negative consequence has been delivered. A common practice is for the teacher to say something like, "Mickaleb, I'd like to visit with you for a moment at the end of the class." Or if the class is engaged, the teacher may approach the student saying, "Mickaleb, glad you are working away here. I'd like to visit with you for a moment."

This visit is designed to encourage students to review the series of events leading to the noncompliant stance. The student would be encouraged to follow requests the first time they are asked, just like the rest of the class. If Step 5 was reached, the teacher would refer to the decision the student made and again provide encouragement to choose to follow the request in the future. Finally, the teacher would encourage the student to ask for help or whatever may be needed to be able to follow requests in the classroom and be successful.

## CHECKLIST AND ACTION PLAN FOR DEFUSING NONCOMPLIANCE AND LIMIT TESTING

Form 6.2, Checklist and Action Plan for Defusing *Noncompliance and Limit Testing* (Appendix I), is intended to be a resource for teachers, so they can evaluate their responses to how noncompliance and limit testing are managed in the classroom. The intent is for teachers to self-evaluate their responses to these behaviors, particularly to determine if they followed the recommended steps. For "yes" responses, the teacher is encouraged to maintain these responses consistently over time. Where "no" responses are recorded, the teacher is encouraged to develop an action plan to ensure the step is followed more reliably on the next occurrence of noncompliance and limit testing.

## APPLICATION OF DEFUSING STEPS ILLUSTRATION FOR NONCOMPLIANCE AND LIMIT TESTING

Earlier in this chapter, an illustration was described for a secondary class in which a student displayed noncompliant behavior (Box 6.1). The situation escalated, taking a considerable amount of teacher time with a strong likelihood that this kind of behavior would be repeated. The recommended steps for defusing noncompliant behavior will now be applied to this example (Box 6.2), followed by some comments.

**Form 6.2**    Checklist and Action Plan for Defusing *Noncompliance and Limit Testing*

## Checklist for Defusing Noncompliance and Limit Testing

### Steps

1. A quick assessment made on occurrence of noncompliance and limit testing behavior to determine
   a. Whether behavior should be managed by teacher or office    YES    NO
   b. Whether prerequisite conditions have been established    YES    NO
      If NO, prerequisite conditions need to be established

2. a. Flow of instruction maintained as a first response    YES    NO
   b. Cooperative students acknowledged first    YES    NO
   c. Delay response to noncompliant behavior    YES    NO

3. Repeat direction privately    YES    NO

4. Disengage, respond to class, and monitor    YES    NO

5. Present request as decision
   a. Establish initial setup    YES    NO
   b. Use nonconfrontational delivery    YES    NO
   c. Present request as decision    YES    NO
   d. Follow through based on student decision    YES    NO

6. Debrief with student at later time    YES    NO

### Action Plan (for Any Items Scored "NO")

_____

_____

_____

_____

_____

_____

_____

## BOX 6.2
## Noncompliance and Limit Testing Illustration
## at Secondary Level

### Recommended Defusing Steps for Managing Noncompliance and Limit Testing

#### Step 1: Assess the Situation

Mr. Pavretti determined that the student's noncompliant behavior was at a level that he should address within the classroom, and he was reasonably sure the student was clear on what was being requested.

#### Step 2: Maintain the Flow of Instruction

Mr. Pavretti was moving around the class checking the progress of his students' work on their assignment, briefly acknowledging their good work and asking if there were any questions. When he approached Anne-Louise's desk, he saw that she had stopped writing. Without pausing, he moved to the next student who was well under way with the assignment. He stopped briefly, saying to her, "Looks like you are well under way. Nice effort." He checked the work of two more students, and then returned to Anne-Louise.

#### Step 3: Repeat Direction Privately

As he approached her, he said quietly, "Anne-Louise, do you have any questions?" Anne-Louise looked at him and did not say anything. Mr. Pavretti then said, "Anne-Louise, the assignment is to summarize the steps for the purchase in one page. So, please continue." She said abruptly, "I am finished, and that's it."

#### Step 4: Disengage, Respond to Class, and Monitor

Mr. Pavretti said no more and moved to other students, acknowledging their work as before. He looked over to Anne-Louise and noticed that she had not resumed her work.

#### Step 5: Provide Focus on Student Decision Making

a.  **Establish Initial Setup.** Mr. Pavretti always spent a little time in his first class of the year explaining his behavioral expectations. He also described his management system by what he does to encourage these expectations and how he addresses problem behavior. He also links these procedures to the schoolwide positive-behavior support endeavors.

b.  **Use a Nonconfrontational Delivery.** Mr. Pavretti approached Anne-Louise deliberately, but not brusquely, and spoke with a flat tone as privately as possible.

c.  **Present the Request as a Decision.** "Anne-Louise. Last time now. If you need help, I will gladly help, but you are asked to complete a page of writing" (*direction*) "or you will be getting a failing grade" (*negative consequence*). "You have a little time left to decide" (*time to decide*). He then moved to nearby students to check their progress (*withdraws*).

d. **Follow Through Based on the Student's Decision.** The teacher looked back and noticed that Anne-Louise had not resumed her work. The papers were collected and subsequently graded. Anne-Louise was given a failing grade.

**Step 6: Debrief With the Student at a Later Time.** A short time after the papers were returned, the teacher told Anne-Louise that he needs to see her at the end of the class. In the visit, he reported that she turned in only two lines of work, earning a failing grade. He mentioned that her earlier work was quite solid, so he wanted to know why she refused to do this assignment. She did not say anything. The teacher then told her that if something else is going on, she needs to let him know, so that he can work with her on it. She didn't say anything. The teacher then said that he hopes this is the exception and that in future assignments she will do her best and earn passing grades.

**Note:** If there was an issue for this student that surfaced, the teacher would probably adjust the grade to an incomplete and give the student a chance to do a makeup. Also, the teacher would encourage her to let him know if something is going on so that he can help as needed. This topic of agitated behavior was addressed in Chapter 5.

**Comments**

1. The teacher worked hard to stay connected to the rest of the class by moving around, checking their progress, responding to them, and clearly delaying responding to the student who was not following the class direction.

2. The teacher was also careful not to become engaged with the student in ongoing discussions (as was depicted in the initial vignette) by staying focused on the class assignment. The teacher maintained calm, respectful, and deliberate contact with the student, especially in delivering the step involving putting the decision on the student to complete the assignment as requested.

3. It was also noted that the teacher tried in the debriefing step to check to see if other issues were operating with the student that may be getting in the way. In effect, the teacher was determining if factors that were addressed in the previous chapter for defusing agitated behavior might be needed. However, the problems and strategies may overlap as depicted in this vignette.

## APPLICATION TO PERSISTENT PROBLEM BEHAVIOR IN THE CLASSROOM

In earlier chapters, it was noted that some problems can begin with off-task behavior (Chapter 2), rule infractions (Chapter 3), and disrespectful behavior (Chapter 4), and they may persist. The defusing strategies for these behaviors will not work unless the student cooperates. At this juncture, in the face of persistent problem behavior, the teacher would use the defusing strategies described in this chapter for addressing noncompliance.

For example, in Chapter 2, Box 2.6, Defusing Off-Task Behavior Vignette for Specialist Class, Physical Education, a situation was described where two students in the physical education class were playing their own game (off-task behavior) instead of the class activity. The teacher followed the defusing steps for addressing off-task behavior, finishing with the direction, "Come over here quickly," and the students kept playing their game and did not join the group (Box 2.6). Now, the teacher would use the steps designed in this chapter for managing noncompliance. The teacher would then approach the two students and say something like, "All right. You are asked to join the group" (*direction*), "or I will have to send you to the office for insubordination and disrupting the class" (*negative consequence*). "You have a few seconds to decide" (*time to decide*). He would then touch base with the rest of the class (*withdraw*), and follow through based on the decision made by the students.

## CHAPTER SUMMARY

Noncompliance and limit testing are behaviors that can become particularly challenging for teachers, and if they are not managed effectively, the teaching–learning process in the classroom can be seriously eroded. Cooperation in the classroom is an essential student behavior for effective teaching.

As with the other common problem behaviors addressed in this book, the key step in defusing noncompliance and limit testing is the teacher's *initial response.* If the teacher directly addresses students' inappropriate behavior (such as whistling, giggling, or chatting when they should be working), the situation will worsen. Similarly, if the teacher initially responds to student challenges (such as, "Make me" or "No way") with a response that directly challenges the student by responding in kind, the situation will become a power struggle with ensuing escalation. The first response, as always, unless the behavior is severe and affecting the safety of others or significantly disrupting the class, is to delay responding to the noncompliant behavior and maintain the flow of instruction. The initial response should always be to the students who are cooperating.

The remaining defusing steps are designed to place the decision for cooperating with the teacher's request *squarely with the student.* The teacher then follows through based on the student's decision.

The steps for defusing noncompliance and limit testing also serve as a bottom line, or final step, for teachers when addressing other problem behaviors in the classroom (such as off-task behavior, rule infractions, disrespect, and agitated behavior). If the students refuse to cooperate with the defusing steps for these behaviors, then the teacher treats the student behavior as noncompliance and utilizes the recommended steps for this behavior.

## PRACTICE EXAMPLE

The reader is invited to review the following classroom vignette and apply the same steps recommended in this chapter for addressing noncompliant and limit testing behavior.

---

### PRACTICE VIGNETTE

#### Noncompliance at Elementary Level

The first-grade students were finishing up a coloring project when the teacher, Ms. Mulaney, announced that they needed to put their materials away and go to their reading groups. The class put their materials away and headed to the reading groups, except for Rodney, who kept coloring. The teacher acknowledged the class for moving so quickly and said to Rodney, "You can finish your project later. It is time for reading now." Rodney said, "No," and kept coloring. The teacher went to him and said, "Look Rodney, put your materials away now, and go to your reading group, or you will have to miss recess." Rodney stiffened somewhat and said, "I don't care," and kept coloring. The teacher began the reading group, and Rodney was kept in at recess.

---

### Response Directions

1. Map the interaction pathway connecting the teacher–student interactions.

2. Identify the main teacher responses that may have contributed to the problem.

3. Identify the main student responses that maintained or worsened the problem.

4. Apply the steps for defusing this noncompliant behavior situation.

5. Note any additional comments.

**Note:** A response key for this problem is provided in Appendix M.

# *Closing Remarks*

There is no question that teachers face many challenges in today's classroom. They not only have to manage multiple responsibilities they also are under scrutiny from the school, district, parents, community, and the public at large. *Hats off to teachers.*

One constant demand is the expectation that teachers can manage and maintain student behavior in ways that lead to safe, orderly, and welcoming environments for all of their students. It has been quite heartening, in this regard, over the past several years, to see the concerted efforts made at local, state, and national levels, to help schools focus on proactive and supportive systems and strategies for establishing desirable student behavior in the schools. This movement has provided teachers with research-based and best-practice strategies for addressing problem behavior and sustaining expected behavior.

Regardless of how systematic and thorough a school may be in developing positive systems for behavior, problems will still arise. Some students may have had a long history of problem behaviors; others may have experienced factors leading to problem behavior outside the school, which spill over to school and classrooms; some may be having the proverbial *bad day*. Basically, teachers will encounter problem behavior in the classroom on a relatively frequent basis.

The common behaviors that teachers may encounter have been identified in this book as *off task, rule infractions, disrespectful behavior, agitated behavior,* and *noncompliance* and *limit testing*. While there are many proactive and supportive strategies for addressing these problem behaviors, one factor is essential and that is the teacher's initial response to the problem behavior. The basic theme of this book is that the teacher's *initial response* will determine to a very large extent whether the behavior is defused or escalated. Central to understanding the importance of the teacher's first response in managing problem behavior is the role of interaction pathways. These pathways track the successive responses between the teacher and students in the context of problem behavior. When teachers respond to problem behavior, they are really responding to the student who is displaying the behavior. Once the teacher makes a response, the student will also respond, leading to another teacher response. It is this back and forth between the teacher and student (interaction pathway) that can result with either an improvement in the situation with on-task behavior (*defused*) or a worsening of the situation with more-serious behavior (*escalated*).

This book has been designed to provide teachers with steps for defusing common problem behaviors in the classroom. These steps have been derived from sound behavioral principles, research, and best practices. The common denominator in the procedures recommended is for teachers to delay responding to students who are displaying problem behavior and make a point of attending to the students who are cooperating. Unfortunately, many teachers are not fluent with this order of responding. Hopefully, this book—with its rationale, procedural steps, and many illustrations—will help teachers review and understand the manner in which they respond to problem behavior. It is a sobering, yet remarkably simple thought for teachers to consider that whether a student's behavior is defused or not depends on their response to that behavior. In particular, the very first response from the teacher is the key. To close, I would like to cite a recent article from the *Los Angeles Times*, which was cited to head the Introduction to this book:

*Educators, administrators and experts say classroom management—the ability to calmly control student behavior so learning can flourish—can make or break a teacher's ability to be successful.*

—Seema Mehta, "Controlling a Classroom Isn't as Easy as ABC,"
*Los Angeles Times*, December 14, 2009

# *Appendices*

**Note:** These appendices may be reproduced or adapted for personal use in the classroom, school, or district.

## APPENDIX A

| Form 2.1 | Prerequisite-Conditions Checklist and Action Plan for *Off-Task Behavior* |

---

### Checklist for Off-Task Behavior

*Scoring Key*

YES   NO   1. Cooperation and on-task behavior are taught as classroom expectations

YES   NO   2. Students have the necessary skills

YES   NO   3. Transitions carefully planned

YES   NO   4. Task requirements clearly presented

YES   NO   5. Adequate time allocated for task completion

YES   NO   6. On-task direction checked (students are "on track")

YES   NO   7. Procedures for requesting assistance established

---

### Action Plan for Items Scored "NO"

_____

_____

_____

_____

_____

_____

_____

_____

_____

_____

---

## APPENDIX B

| Form 2.2 | Checklist and Action Plan for Defusing *Off-Task Behavior* |
|---|---|

### Checklist for Defusing Off-Task Behavior

**Steps**

1. A quick assessment made on occurrence of off-task behavior to determine

    a. Whether student has the prerequisite skills to complete the task    YES    NO

    b. Whether off-task behavior was severe safety-wise or disruption-wise    YES    NO

       If YES, crisis or emergency procedures followed    YES    NO

       If NO, off-task defusing steps below followed    YES    NO

2. a. Flow of instruction maintained as a first response    YES    NO

    b. Off-task students acknowledged briefly if on-task behavior followed    YES    NO

3. a. On-task students acknowledged as second response    YES    NO

    b. No response made to off-task students    YES    NO

    c. Off-task students acknowledged briefly if on-task behavior followed    YES    NO

4. Redirection prompt was delivered as third response with features

    a. Strong focus on required task    YES    NO

    b. Brief language or use of gestures employed    YES    NO

    c. No response at all made to student's off-task behavior    YES    NO

    d. Remind student of procedures for assistance or offer to help    YES    NO

5. a. If student cooperates, displaying on-task behavior, brief acknowledgment is delivered    YES    NO

    b. If student does not cooperate, move to procedures for noncompliance and limit testing from Chapter 6    YES    NO

### Action Plan (for Any Items Scored "NO")

_____

_____

_____

_____

## APPENDIX C

**Form 3.1**  Prerequisite-Conditions Checklist and Action Plan for *Rule Infractions*

### Checklist for Rule Infractions

*Scoring Key*

YES    The item is clearly in place

NO    The item is not in place, or there is uncertainty whether it is in place or not

**Items**

YES    NO    1. Schoolwide rules taught and established by faculty

YES    NO    2. Classroom rules and expectations systematically taught

YES    NO    3. Students frequently acknowledged for following classroom rules

YES    NO    4. Practices in place to monitor and review the rules

### Action Plan for Items Scored "NO"

_____

_____

_____

_____

_____

_____

_____

_____

_____

_____

## APPENDIX D

**Form 3.2**   Checklist and Action Plan for Defusing *Rule Infractions*

### Checklist for Defusing Rule Infractions

**Steps**

1. A quick assessment made on occurrence of rule infraction to determine

   a. Whether student knows the rule or expectation      YES    NO
      If NO, rule needs to be taught or clarified

   b. Whether the rule infraction was severe safety-wise or disruption-wise   YES    NO
      If YES, crisis or emergency procedures followed      YES    NO
      If NO, defusing steps below followed      YES    NO

2. a. Flow of instruction maintained as a first response      YES    NO
   b. On-task students acknowledged      YES    NO

3. a. Students following rule acknowledged      YES    NO
   b. No immediate response to student exhibiting rule infraction      YES    NO

4. Rule clarified and restated      YES    NO

5. Student directly asked to take care of the problem      YES    NO

6. Options presented if student does nor (or cannot) initiate response      YES    NO

7. a. If student cooperates and addresses problem, brief
      acknowledgment delivered      YES    NO
   b. If student does not cooperate and refuses to address problem,
      procedures for noncompliance from Chapter 6 implemented      YES    NO

### Action Plan (for Any Items Scored "NO")

_____

_____

_____

_____

_____

## APPENDIX E

| Form 4.1 | Prerequisite-Conditions Checklist and Action Plan for *Disrespectful Behavior* |
|---|---|

### Checklist for Disrespectful Behavior

*Scoring Key*

|  | |
|---|---|
| YES | The item is clearly in place |
| NO | The item is not in place, or there is uncertainty whether it is in place or not |

**Items**

| | | |
|---|---|---|
| YES | NO | 1. Respectful behavior is taught as a schoolwide expectation |
| | | 2. The following factors are addressed schoolwide as necessary |
| YES | NO | a. Issues with diversity |
| YES | NO | b. Clarification of respect versus friendship |
| YES | NO | c. Teachers model respectful behavior |
| YES | NO | d. Respect is the norm between faculty |
| YES | NO | 3. Students are frequently acknowledged for showing respectful behavior |
| YES | NO | 4. Practices are in place to regularly monitor and review respectful-behavior practices |

### Action Plan for Items Scored "NO"

_____

_____

_____

_____

_____

## APPENDIX F

**Form 4.2**   Checklist and Action Plan for Defusing *Disrespectful Behavior*

---

### Checklist for Defusing Disrespectful Behavior

**Steps**

1. A quick assessment made on occurrence of disrespectful behavior to determine
   a. Whether prerequisite conditions have been met          YES    NO
      If NO, prerequisite conditions need to be established
   b. Whether behavior warrants office referral               YES    NO
      If YES, follow with office referral
      If NO, defusing steps below followed

2. a. Flow of instruction maintained as a first response      YES    NO
   b. On-task students acknowledged                           YES    NO

3. Studiously avoids reacting to disrespectful behavior       YES    NO

4. Pauses and disengages                                      YES    NO

5. Makes measured response to student's behavior
   a. Uses student's name                                     YES    NO
   b. Names student's behavior                                YES    NO
   c. Delivers consequence                                    YES    NO
   d. Redirects student to class activity                     YES    NO

6. Debriefs with student at later time                        YES    NO

---

### Action Plan (for Any Items Scored "NO")

_____

_____

_____

_____

_____

---

## APPENDIX G

**Form 5.1**    Checklist and Action Plan for Defusing *Agitated Behavior*

---

### Checklist for Defusing Agitated Behavior

**Steps**

1. A quick assessment made on occurrence of agitated behavior to determine

   a. Whether behavior should be managed by teacher or office          YES     NO

   b. Whether behavior is frequent, warranting more-intensive
      intervention                                                     YES     NO
      If YES, initiate more intensive plan
      If NO, defusing steps below followed

2. a. Flow of instruction maintained as a first response              YES     NO
   b. On-task students acknowledged                                   YES     NO

3. Signs of agitation identified                                      YES     NO

   *Increases in Behavior*

   ❑ Darting eyes
   ❑ Busy hands
   ❑ Moving in and out of groups
   ❑ Off-task and on-task cycle
   ❑ Easily irritated by other students
   ❑ Other

   *Decreases in Behavior*

   ❑ Staring into space
   ❑ Veiled eyes
   ❑ Nonconversational language
   ❑ Contained hands
   ❑ Withdrawal
   ❑ Readily attributes blame
   ❑ Other

4. Use calming strategies                                             YES     NO

   ❑ Teacher empathy
   ❑ Helping student focus on class activity
   ❑ Providing space
   ❑ Present options
   ❑ Providing assurances and additional time
   ❑ Permit preferred activities
   ❑ Teacher proximity
   ❑ Independent activities

❑ Passive activities
❑ Movement activities
❑ Student self-management
❑ Other

| | | |
|---|---|---|
| 5. Monitor accommodations | YES | NO |
| 6. Debrief with student at later time | YES | NO |

**Action Plan (for Any Items Scored "NO")**

_____

_____

_____

_____

_____

_____

_____

_____

_____

_____

_____

_____

_____

_____

_____

## APPENDIX H

| Form 6.1 | Prerequisite-Conditions Checklist and Action Plan for *Noncompliance and Limit Testing* |

### Checklist for Noncompliance and Limit Testing

*Scoring Key*

YES    NO    1. Direction delivered by school authority

YES    NO    2. Following directions taught as classroom expectation

YES    NO    3. Directions are understood

YES    NO    4. Students have ability to fulfill directions

YES    NO    5. Directions delivered positively

YES    NO    6. Students' attention secured

### Action Plan (for Any Items Scored "NO")

_____

_____

_____

_____

_____

_____

_____

_____

_____

_____

_____

_____

_____

## APPENDIX I

**Form 6.2**   Checklist and Action Plan for Defusing *Noncompliance and Limit Testing*

---

### Checklist for Defusing Noncompliance and Limit Testing

**Steps**

1. A quick assessment made on occurrence of noncompliance and limit testing behavior to determine
   a. Whether behavior should be managed by teacher or office     YES     NO
   b. Whether prerequisite conditions have been established     YES     NO
   If NO, prerequisite conditions need to be established

2. a. Flow of instruction maintained as a first response     YES     NO
   b. Cooperative students acknowledged first     YES     NO
   c. Delay response to noncompliant behavior     YES     NO

3. Repeat direction privately     YES     NO

4. Disengage, respond to class, and monitor     YES     NO

5. Present request as decision     YES     NO
   a. Establish initial setup     YES     NO
   b. Use nonconfrontational delivery     YES     NO
   c. Present request as decision     YES     NO
   d. Follow through based on student decision     YES     NO

6. Debrief with student at later time     YES     NO

---

### Action Plan (for Any Items Scored "NO")

_____

_____

_____

_____

_____

_____

_____

## APPENDIX J

### Response Key to Practice Example on Rule Infractions, Chapter 3

| Rule Infraction in Specialist Class, Art | | |
|---|---|---|
| **Vignette** | **Interaction Pathway** | |
| | **Teacher Response** | **Student Response** |
| The art teacher, Ms. Rawinsky, has a routine where the students have to have all the materials on their table before they begin to draw. She has found this procedure is more efficient, causing less traffic during class, fewer accidents, and she can readily track what is needed. She reminded and explained this rule at the beginning of art class. | The teacher explains procedures and notices Heather starts to draw without getting all the materials, so reminds her to follow the procedures | |
| | | Says she wants to draw first because she may spill paint on her drawing |
| One student, Heather, collected an art sheet and began to draw immediately, without getting the painting material. | Directed student to stop drawing and get the rest of materials | |
| The teacher worked her way over to Heather and reminded her that she needs to get all of the materials for class before she starts to draw. Heather exclaimed that she needs to draw first so that she doesn't spill any paint on her drawing. | | Keeps drawing, and does not respond to teacher's directions |
| The teacher said quite clearly that Heather needs to stop drawing and get the rest of the materials. Heather kept drawing. The teacher then gave her a choice of getting the rest of the material or Heather would have to go to the time-out area and read. Heather keeps drawing, ignoring the ultimatum. Ms. Rawinsky then sends her to the time-out area. | Delivers ultimatum to follow directions, or she will be sent to the time-out area | |
| | | Keeps drawing |
| | Directs her to the time-out area | |

### Analysis of Teacher Responses to Breaking Rule

- The teacher stops attending to other students and focuses on Heather.
- The teacher gives the student a direction in the context of a rule infraction.
- The teacher does not address student's concern about spilling paint on her drawing.
- The teacher gives an ultimatum, which could readily lead to a power struggle.
- The teacher follows through on procedures for dealing with rule breaking, sending the student to the time-out area.

### Analysis of Student Responses for Rule Infraction

- The student receives public attention for not following the rules.
- The student may be upset that the teacher did not hear her concern about spilling paint on her drawing.
- The student causes class to be disrupted.
- The student is sent to time-out area and misses some or all of the art-class activity.

## Defusing Rule Infraction Vignette for Specialist Class, Art

### Recommended Defusing Steps for Managing Rule Infraction

#### Step 1: Assess the Situation

Ms. Rawinsky assumed the students knew the procedures because, even though she has each class once a week, she always begins the class by going over her rules and procedures. She also concluded that the student's rule infraction was one that she should deal with directly, in the art room.

#### Step 2: Maintain the Flow of Instruction

Ms. Rawinsky saw that Heather went straight to drawing without getting the painting materials, but she moved around the class checking to see that the students had all their materials and acknowledged them for responding promptly.

#### Step 3: Attend to On-Task Students Who Are Following the Rules

Ms. Rawinsky announces to the class that she is pleased to see that the students are taking care of business, getting all their materials, and setting up their tables for their art project.

#### Step 4: Clarify the Rule or Expectation

Once the class is under way with their drawing, the teacher approaches Heather and says privately, "Heather, we need to get all our materials for the class before we start

*(Continued)*

(Continued)

drawing. I went over this a few minutes ago." Heather utters that she is afraid of spilling paint on her drawing, so she needs to draw first. The teacher explains that the tables are large, and you can set the painting materials aside, and she tells Heather to look how Rose (next to her) had her materials laid out.

### Step 5: Explicitly Request the Student to Take Care of the Problem

She then says, "Heather, we need to get all materials first, so please take care of that." She then goes to other students while keeping an eye on Heather by glancing over to her space.

### Step 6: Present Problem-Solving Options If Needed

In this case, the procedures are clear cut, so options are not critical for this particular rule infraction.

### Step 7: Follow Through Based on Student's Response

The student heads to the paint materials area, gathers what is needed, and places them on her table away from her drawing. The teacher acknowledges her cooperation and remarks that the arrangement on her desk should be fine.

### Comments

1. In this vignette, the teacher clearly focused on the majority of the students who were following her procedures as her first response.

2. The teacher clarified the rule in a matter-of-fact manner and reminded the student of the explanations at the start of class.

3. The teacher did not dismiss or ignore the student's concern about spilling paint on her drawing. Rather, she showed her how to solve that problem and returned to the initial need to follow the class procedures.

4. After the teacher redirected Heather to get all the materials, she went to the rest of the class, leaving Heather alone to some extent to make her decision to follow the procedures or not. This step helps her save face and allows her to process the request from the teacher.

5. The situation, in this case, was defused as the student followed the procedures, met her needs of not spilling paint on her drawing, and did not miss any art time.

## APPENDIX K

Response Key to Practice Example on Disrespectful Behavior, Chapter 4

| BOX 4.1 Disrespectful Behavior at Kindergarten/Elementary Level | | |
|---|---|---|
| **Vignette** | **Interaction Pathway** | |
| | **Teacher Response** | **Student Response** |
| Ms. Sandursky, a kindergarten teacher, notices that two of her students are engaged in an argument over who should be playing with a particular toy during free time. She approaches the two students and says, "Rosalind and Tamara, listen to me, please. We need to share these toys." Rosalind interrupts the teacher, saying, "No. Go away. It's my turn," and makes a grab at the toy. The teacher takes the toy and tells Rosalind she shouldn't interrupt like that. Rosalind shouts, "It's not fair. I hate you." The teacher quickly takes her by the arm and says very firmly, "Listen. Don't you talk to me like that." Rosalind, starts to scream and throws herself on the floor. | Notices two students arguing over a toy during free time, and tells students they need to share | |
| | | One student interrupts, tells teacher to go away, that it's her turn, and tries to grab the toy |
| | Takes the toy, and tells student she should not interrupt like that | |
| | | Says it's not fair and, "I hate you" |
| | Quickly grabs student's arm, telling her not to talk to her like that | |
| | | Student screams and throws herself on the floor |

### Analysis of Teacher Responses to the Disrespectful Behavior

- The teacher moves quickly to the two arguing students to solve the conflict.
- The teacher provides the two students arguing with immediate attention.
- The teacher uses sharing as the solution to the problem—one of the goals for free time activities.
- The teacher addresses interruption versus the disrespectful behavior when the child tells her to go away.
- The teacher reacts very quickly to the student's next disrespectful statement of "I hate you" by grabbing her arm and taking the toy.
- The teacher provided a personal reaction by saying, "Don't you talk to me like that."

### Analysis of Student Responses for Disrespectful Behavior

- The student secured teacher attention through arguing with another student over a toy during free time.
- The student interrupts the teacher and tells her to go away (disrespectful behavior) when the teacher said they needed to share.
- The student's behavior is escalated, becoming more disrespectful—when the teacher tells her not to interrupt—trying to grab the toy and shouting, "I hate you" (more disrespectful behavior).
- The student starts screaming and throws herself on the floor when the teacher took the toy, saying not to talk to her like that (escalated and disruptive behavior).

---

### BOX 4.4
### Defusing Disrespectful Behavior Vignette for Kindergarten and Elementary Level

### Recommended Defusing Steps for Managing Disrespectful Behavior

#### Step 1: Assess the Situation

Ms. Sandursky checked YES for all items in Form 4.1, Prerequisite-Conditions Checklist and Action Plan for *Disrespectful Behavior*. Also, she determined that the level of behavior warranted the problem to be dealt with in the classroom versus needing to make an office referral.

### Step 2: Maintain the Flow of Instruction

Ms. Sandursky moved toward the two students who were arguing, but on her way she acknowledged other students who were productively engaged in activities and interacting appropriately. She made sure this was her first response before she addressed the two students who were arguing. She also looked around the room to quickly monitor the rest of the class.

### Step 3: Studiously Avoid Reacting to the Disrespectful Behavior

The teacher noted that one of the students was disrespectful in telling her to "go away" and decided to delay responding to the behavior. The teacher also tried not to show annoyance, which could be easy to do given a five-year-old told her to go away.

### Step 4: Pause and Disengage

Ms. Sandursky looked at Rosalind, then at the other student without saying anything (aware that she was not going to respond quickly to Rosalind's disrespectful behavior). The teacher looked to the students nearby who were playing appropriately with their games, telling them in a very pleasant tone that she appreciates how nicely they are playing. She then looked at the other student with Rosalind and asked her to go to another station or find another toy. This student had not said anything. The teacher acknowledged her when she cooperated with this direction.

### Step 5: Address the Student's Behavior in a Measured Manner

The teacher now uses a fairly flat tone (different than the tone used to acknowledge the other students for playing appropriately) and says, "Rosalind" (uses student's name), looking at her, pausing slightly to secure her attention, "What you just said, telling me to go away, is very disrespectful" (names the student's behavior). "We can't talk like that, so you will have to miss the rest of free time and go to the quiet area" (delivers consequence).

The teacher acknowledges Rosalind briefly for following the direction of going to the quiet area.

Following the free-time session, the teacher tells Rosalind to join her reading group and that she needs to see her later (redirects her to class activity and acknowledges cooperation).

### Step 6: Debrief With the Student at a Later Time

During the transition at the end of the reading group the teacher catches Rosalind and tells her she just wants to talk a little about the problem with the toy and with what she said to the teacher. Ms. Sandusrsky told Rosalind that the teacher must go to students when there are problems and that the student cannot tell the teacher to go away. Also, in free time, if two students want a toy, then they have to share and take turns. If you and the other child cannot work it out, then you have to come to me.

## Comments

1. The teacher made sure that her first response to the two students arguing was to ignore them and acknowledge the rest of the class for cooperating with the class activity, free time.

2. The teacher addressed the initial disrespectful behavior versus reacting to the subsequent disrespectful behaviors as in the original vignette.

3. By following the steps, the teacher was able to arrest the problem at the first instance of disrespectful behavior and prevent subsequent escalation.

4. The instance was followed up so that the student could more fully understand the teacher's actions, and problem-solving strategies were presented to prevent future problems.

## APPENDIX L

Response Key to Practice Example on Agitated Behavior, Chapter 5

| BOX 5.2 Agitated-Behavior Vignette at Secondary Level | | |
| --- | --- | --- |
| Vignette | Interaction Pathway | |
| | Teacher Response | Student Response |

During independent work in math, students are expected to complete problems that were assigned in the previous class. One student, Roland, is sitting slouched in his seat, feet stretched out, head down, staring at the floor, and looking very serious. The teacher, Ms. Hendley, approached him saying, "Roland, it is time to get started on your math." Roland, without raising his head, said loudly, "I'm done." The teacher looked over his shoulder and saw that he completed some of the problems, but not all of them. "Roland, you have made a good start, but please get on with it, and finish up the assignment." Roland rounded his shoulders, put his head down, and said, "I am not doing this stuff twice." The teacher said, "If you need help let me know; otherwise, if you don't finish it, your grades will be down." Roland said, "Pshaw!" and waved his arm to dismiss the teacher. The teacher moved away to another student.

**Teacher Response**

Set independent work in math for class to finish assignment

Approaches student prompting him to get started on his math

Checks work, comments on good start, but tells Roland he needs to finish

**Student Response**

Most students are working except for Roland, who is just sitting at his desk

Responds loudly, "I'm done"

Showed further agitation, rounding shoulders and putting head down, saying, "I'm not doing this twice"

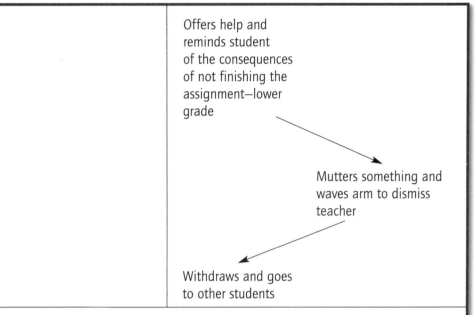

Offers help and reminds student of the consequences of not finishing the assignment—lower grade

Mutters something and waves arm to dismiss teacher

Withdraws and goes to other students

## Analysis of Teacher Responses to Agitated Behavior

- The teacher responds to the student who is off task first.
- The teacher proceeds in a businesslike manner, encouraging the student to get working but does not address the body language signs that suggest the student is agitated (head down, staring at the floor, and feet outstretched).
- The teacher checks work, makes positive response to work student has completed, encourages student to complete assignment, ignores student's loud response, and again does not address the student's escalating agitation.
- The teacher notifies student of the consequence for work not done—receiving a lower grade.
- The teacher realizes that the student is not going to do the work and withdraws to other students.
- Overall, the teacher used normal procedures for managing off-task behavior and did not address at any stage the student's agitation. Moreover, the teacher stayed with the normal procedures when the student's behavior was escalating.

## Analysis of Student Responses for Agitated Behavior

- The student was first to receive teacher attention in the class for being off task
- The student probably drew the attention of nearby students.
- By shouting, the student indicated an escalation of behavior. The teacher's encouragement served as a cue for worse behavior.
- The student refused to begin the work, saying that he is not doing it twice. Also, the student indicated that he was not seeking or responsive to a clarification on what work needed to be done.
- The student reacted further by waving his arm at the teacher and mumbling something disrespectful, indicating that the teacher's reminder of the possibility of a lower grade served as a threat.
- The student was ultimately left alone, which was what he wanted in the first place, meaning that his whole chain of escalating responses was reinforced.

## BOX 5.5
### Defusing Agitated Behavior Vignette for Secondary Level

## Recommended Defusing Steps for Managing Agitated Behavior

### Step 1: Assess the Situation

The teacher, Ms. Hendley, determined that the Roland's behavior should be managed in the classroom. Some teachers may conclude that Roland's behavior ended up being quite noncompliant and disrespectful and should warrant an office referral. Ms. Hendley was of the opinion that Roland was not disturbing the class and that the natural consequences of a lower grade were sufficient to address both his refusal to finish the work and his disrespectful behavior.

Ms. Hendley also determined that Roland's behavior was something she had not observed before and at this stage did not need additional follow up.

### Step 2: Maintain the Flow of Instruction

Ms. Hendley noticed that Roland was not working, and she made a concerted effort to acknowledge the students who were working on their math assignment by moving around the room, checking their work, and asking if there were any questions. No response was made to Roland at this stage.

### Step 3: Identify Signs of Agitation

Ms. Hendley could see immediately that Roland was agitated. His body language was quite clear in the way he sat slouched in his chair, with his feet stretched out on the floor. He was staring at the floor and had a serious look on his face. It was obvious he had shut down.

### Step 4: Use Calming Activities

Ms. Hendley decided she needed to take deliberate steps to bring Roland out of his shell and help him to resume his work. After she had acknowledged the class for their on-task behavior, she approached Roland and said, "Roland. How are we doing on this math assignment?"(prompt to *help student focus on class assignment*). She leaned a little closer to him and said quietly, "You don't look very comfortable today. Is everything all right?" (*teacher empathy*). Ms. Hendley, paused a moment, looked around the room to quickly check the class, and then turned back to Roland, noticing that he had tensed up more. She then said, "Why don't you sit for a little while, and I will be back shortly" (*providing space*).

The teacher then moved around the room checking the students' work, asking if there were any questions, and reminding them of the activity following completion of the math assignment. In a few minutes, she returned to Roland, checked his work without any conversation, and noticed he had completed a few problems and had

*(Continued)*

(Continued)

stopped halfway through. She took his pen and said, "Let's look at number six here." She wrote the number six on his notebook and handed him the pen. Roland sat up a little and took the pen (*helping student focus on class activity*). "Good," the teacher said, "Now, let's see if we can get number six done." She waited while he began to work on this problem and said, "Great, you are up and running. Let me know if you need any help." She then moved to other students.

### Step 5: Monitor Accommodations

Ms. Hendley was aware that she gave Roland more attention and assistance than the other students. She monitored him for the rest of the period to see if he shut down again. He was able to continue working, and she made brief contact with him during the remainder of the period.

### Step 6: Debrief With the Student at a Later Time

Ms. Hendley approached Roland toward the end of the period and said to him as privately as possible, "I'd like to catch you before you leave class for a minute, please." When Roland came to her at the end of class, she said, "Roland, thanks for remembering to see me. I want to tell you how impressed I was to see you knuckle down and get your work done. Thanks." She then paused and smiled, "I also want you to know that if you get stuck to please ask for help. Or, if there is anything else you need, please let me know. I will try to help." The teacher did not want to probe too hard, but wanted to let the student know she was there if he needed her support.

### Comments

1. This vignette unfolded in a dramatically different fashion when the teacher addressed the student's agitation compared to the original vignette where the teacher held her ground and challenged the student to get his work completed.

2. The teacher clearly recognized the student's agitation and quietly eased the student back to work.

3. The student picked up that the teacher was not his adversary and that she was trying to be caring as well as helping him to get his work completed.

4. The teacher was aware that this was the first time she had seen this level of agitation from her student, so in the debriefing visit she simply made herself available to provide support as needed without being too pushy or nosy about his issues.

## APPENDIX M

## Response Key to Practice Example on Noncompliance and Limit Testing, Chapter 6

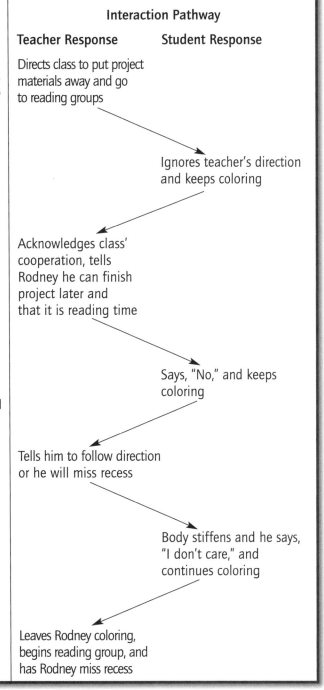

### BOX 6.3
### Noncompliance and Limit-Testing Vignette
### at Kindergarten and Elementary Level

| Vignette | Interaction Pathway | |
|---|---|---|
| | Teacher Response | Student Response |

The first-grade students were finishing up a coloring project when the teacher, Ms. Mulaney, announced that they needed to put their materials away and go to their reading groups. The class put their materials away and headed to the reading groups except for Rodney, who kept coloring. The teacher acknowledged the class for moving so quickly and said to Rodney, "You can finish your project later. It is time for reading now." Rodney said, "No," and kept coloring. The teacher went to him and said, "Look, Rodney, put your materials away now, and go to your reading group, or you will have to miss recess." Rodney stiffened somewhat and said, "I don't care," and kept coloring. The teacher began the reading group, and Rodney was kept in at recess.

**Teacher Response**

Directs class to put project materials away and go to reading groups

Acknowledges class' cooperation, tells Rodney he can finish project later and that it is reading time

Tells him to follow direction or he will miss recess

Leaves Rodney coloring, begins reading group, and has Rodney miss recess

**Student Response**

Ignores teacher's direction and keeps coloring

Says, "No," and keeps coloring

Body stiffens and he says, "I don't care," and continues coloring

## Analysis of Teacher Responses to Noncompliance and Limit Testing

- The teacher acknowledged class for cooperating with the direction to switch to reading and delayed responding to Rodney.
- The teacher reacted quickly to the student saying, "No." Such a quick and focused response from the teacher of taking up the challenge may have reinforced the student's defiance.
- The teacher gave Rodney an option for finishing his project later and stayed with the direction of putting things away and joining the group.
- The teacher gave the student a choice between following the direction or missing recess.
- The teacher may have noticed the student's body stiffening and so decided to back off.
- The teacher left the student to continue drawing and had Rodney miss recess.

## Analysis of Student Responses for Noncompliance and Limit Testing

- The student ignored teacher's initial direction and kept coloring.
- The student did not respond to the opportunity to finishing his project later.
- The student's noncompliance became more overt when he responded with "no" to teacher direction.
- The student's body language (stiffening) indicated more resistance, and he dismissed the consequences of missing recess ("I don't care").
- Overall, the student became more resistant as the teacher tried to follow through with the direction.
- The need to keep coloring and finish the project was more important to the student than following the teacher's directions, going to reading, and missing recess.

---

### BOX 6.4
### Defusing Noncompliance and Limit-Testing Behavior Vignette for Kindergarten and Elementary Level

### Recommended Defusing Steps for Managing Noncompliance and Limit Testing

#### Step 1: Assess the Situation

The teacher determined that the student's behavior was one that should be managed in the classroom. In addition, she believed that she had been quite systematic in teaching cooperation as an important expectation in the classroom. She also determined that the student had heard the direction and was quite capable of following the request.

### Step 2: Maintain the Flow of Instruction

The first response from the teacher was to acknowledge the class for cooperating with the direction to switch to reading, realizing that it is a transition step. She also delayed responding to the student who did not follow the direction. The teacher then gave the class a direction to open their reading books to the "Little Acorn" story and begin to look at all the things in the picture on page 2.

### Step 3: Repeat Direction Privately

Once the class was involved with this activity, the teacher approached the student privately and told him that the coloring could be completed later and that he needed to switch to reading. If he cooperated, she would acknowledge him and continue with the reading lesson for the class. If he did not cooperate and defiantly said, "No," as in the original vignette, the teacher would proceed to Step 4.

### Step 4: Disengage, Respond to Class, and Monitor

As soon as the student utters, "No," the teacher pauses. The pause prevents a quick response, which is likely to reinforce the student's challenging situation. Following the pause, the teacher says to the student, "Just a second," and moves to the class, saying something related to the lesson, such as, "Good. I see you are all looking at that picture. In a moment, we will say more about it." The teacher then looks over at the student, Rodney. If he has moved to his reading group, he would be acknowledged briefly. If not, the teacher would proceed to Step 5.

### Step 5: Provide Focus on Student Decision Making

a. **Establish Initial Setup.** Ms. Mulaney, in the first week of every school year, carefully goes over her expectations, how she encourages desirable behavior, and how she deals with problem behavior. She also reviewed these procedures at regular intervals throughout the year. She firmly believes that good behavior needs to be taught. As part of this teaching package, she would explain to the class the steps she takes when students persist with problem behavior and become noncompliant and defiant (the steps below).

b. **Use a Nonconfrontational Delivery.** Ms. Mulaney returned to her student, Rodney, approached him in a calm manner, bent down in front of him (versus towering over him or approaching him from behind), and used a plain or matter-of-fact tone.

c. **Present the Request as a Decision.** "Rodney, listen carefully, please. You are asked to put your coloring materials away and move to your reading group" (*direction*). "Or, you will have to miss recess" (*negative consequence*). "You have a few seconds to decide" (*time to decide*). Ms. Mulaney stood up, then moved to other students (*withdraws*).

d. **Follow Through Based on the Student's Decision.** Rodney mumbled under his breath, put the materials away, and moved slowly to his group. Ms. Mulaney was talking to the class about the picture and without pausing moved to Rodney and said very quietly and privately, "Thanks for joining the group," then continued with the discussion on the picture.

### Step 6: Debrief With the Student at a Later Time

When the class was reading silently, Ms Mulaney approached Rodney and said, "Good, Rodney, I am glad you are doing your reading. Listen, earlier you were very slow to join the group and even said 'no' when I asked you the second time. So, let's not have that again. We can work something out with your coloring, but you must follow the class directions. OK?" She asked him if he had any question, and he shook his head. She then told him to keep up the good work with his reading and moved around the room.

### Comments

1. The teacher was well aware that Rodney was fully engaged with his coloring and would be slow to cooperate with the next direction. However, the teacher persisted with the steps for addressing his initial noncompliance, resulting with him following the class direction.

2. The teacher made good use of delaying responding to the student's noncompliance by pausing, going to other students in the class and, above all, not getting engaged with him. By calm and deliberate persistence, she was able to prompt him to follow the class direction and move from his preferred activity.

# *References*

Algozzine, B., & Kay, P. (2001). *Preventing problem behaviors: A handbook of successful prevention strategies.* Thousand Oaks, CA: Corwin.

Becker, W. C. (1986). *Applied psychology for teachers: A behavioral cognitive approach.* Chicago: Science Research Associates, Inc.

Bellamy, G. T., Horner, R. H., & Inman, D. P. (1979). *Vocational habilitation of severely retarded adults.* Austin, TX: Pro-Ed.

Brophy, J. (1998). *Advances in research on teaching: Expectations in the classroom Vol. 7.* New York: Jai Press/Elsevier.

Carr, J. E., & Shabani, D. B. (2005). *Maintenance.* In M. Hersen, A. M. Gross, & R. S. Drabman (Eds.), *Encyclopedia of behavior modification and cognitive behavior therapy Vol. 2* (pp. 897–901). Thousand Oaks, CA: Sage.

Carr, J., & Wilder, D. A. (2004). *Functional assessment and intervention: A guide to understanding behavior* (2nd ed.). Homewood, IL: High Tide Press.

Cawley, J., Hayden, S., Cade, E., & Baker-Kroczynski, S. (2002). Including students with disabilities into the general education science classroom. *Council for Exceptional Children, 68*(4), 423–425.

Cipani, E., & Schock, K. (2007). *Functional behavioral assessment, diagnosis, and treatment: A complete system for education and mental health settings.* New York: Springer.

Colvin, G. (2004). *Managing the cycle of acting-out behavior in the classroom.* Eugene, OR: Behavior Associates.

Colvin, G. (2007). *7 steps for developing a proactive schoolwide discipline plan: A guide for principals and leadership teams.* Thousand Oaks, CA: Corwin.

Colvin, G. (2009). *Managing noncompliance and defiance in the classroom: A road map for teachers, specialists, and behavior support teams.* Thousand Oaks, CA: Corwin.

Colvin, G., & Lazar, M. (1997). *The effective elementary classroom: Managing for success.* Longmont, CO: Sopris West.

Cooper, C. R., Chavira, G., & Mena, D. D. (2005). From pipelines to partnerships: A synthesis if research on how diverse families, schools, and communities support children's pathways through school. *Journal of Education for Students Placed at Risk, 10*(4), 407–432.

Cooper, J. O., Heron, T. E., & Heward, W. L. (2007). *Applied behavior analysis* (2nd ed.). Upper Saddle River, NJ: Pearson Education.

Cotton, K. (2000). *The schooling practices that matter most.* Alexandria, VA: Association for Supervision and Curriculum Development.

Darch, C. B., & Kame'enui, E. J. (2004). *Instructional classroom management: A proactive approach to classroom management* (2nd ed.). Upper Saddle River, NJ: Pearson Education.

Ehrenreich, J. T., & Fisak, B. J., Jr. (2005). *Anxiety management.* In M. Hersen, A. M. Gross, & R. S. Drabman (Eds.), *Encyclopedia of behavior modification and cognitive behavior therapy, Vol. 2* (pp. 662–666). Thousand Oaks, CA: Sage.

Eisenberg, M. E., Neumark-Sztainer, D., & Story, M. (2003). *Archives of Pediatrics and Adolescent Medicine, 157,* 733–738.

Evertson, C. M., Emmer, E. T., Clements, B. S., & Worsham, M. E. (1994). *Classroom management for elementary teachers* (3rd ed.). Boston: Allyn & Bacon.

Henze, R., Norte, E., Sather, S. E., Walker, E., & Katz, A. (2002). *Leading for diversity: How school leaders promote positive interethnic relations.* Thousand Oaks, CA: Corwin.

Lane, K. L., Wehby, J. H., & Cooley, C. (2006). Teacher expectations of students' classroom behavior across grade span: Which social skills are necessary for success. *Exceptional Children, 72*(2), 153–167.

Liaupsin, C. (2005). *Teaching schoolwide expectations.* In M. Hersen, G. Sugai, & R. Horner (Eds.), *Encyclopedia of behavior modification and cognitive behavior therapy, Vol. 3* (pp. 1569–1572). Thousand Oaks, CA: Sage.

March, J. K., & Peters, K. H. (2007). *Designing instruction: Making best practices work in standards-based classrooms.* Thousand Oaks, CA: Corwin.

May, S., Ard, W., Todd, A. W., Horner, R. H., Glasgow, A., Sugai, G., & Sprague, J. (2003). *Schoolwide information system.* Eugene: Educational and Community Supports, University of Oregon.

Mayer, G. R. (2005). *Schoolwide discipline.* In M. Hersen, G. Sugai, & R. Horner (Eds.), *Encyclopedia of behavior modification and cognitive behavior therapy, Vol. 3* (pp. 1496–1506). Thousand Oaks, CA: Sage.

Mehta, S. (2009, December 14). Controlling a classroom isn't as easy as ABC. *Los Angeles Times.* Retrieved January 23, 2010, from http://articles.latimes.com/2009/dec/14/local/la-me-classroom-control14-2009dec14.

Metzler, C., Biglan, A., Rusby, J., & Sprague, J. (2001). Evaluation of a comprehensive behavior management program to improve schoolwide positive behavior support. *Education and Treatment of Children, 24*(4), 448–479.

Moran, C., Stobbe, J., Baron, W., Miller, J., & Moir, E. (2008). *Keys to the elementary classroom: A new teacher's guide to the first month of school* (3rd ed.). Thousand Oaks, CA: Corwin.

Office of Special Education and Supports, Center on Positive and Behavioral Interventions and Supports. (2004). *Schoolwide and behavior support implementer's blueprint and support assessment.* Eugene: University of Oregon.

O'Neill, R. E., Horner, R. H., Albin, R. W., Storey, K., Sprague, J., & Newton, J. S. (1997). *Functional assessment and program development for problem behavior: A practical handbook* (2nd ed.). Pacific Grove, CA: Brooks/Cole.

Roberts, W. B., Jr. (2006). *Bullying from both sides: Strategic interventions for working with bullies and victims.* Thousand Oaks, CA: Corwin.

Schoenfield, G., & Morris, R. J. (2009). *Cognitive-behavioral treatment for childhood anxiety disorders: Exemplary programs.* In M. Mayer, R. VanAcker, J. Lochman, & F. Gresham (Eds.), *Cognitive-behavioral interventions for emotional and behavioral disorders: School-based practice* (pp. 204–232). New York: Guilford Press.

Scott, T. M. (2007). Issues of personal dignity and social validity in schoolwide systems of positive behavior support. *Journal of Positive Behavior Interventions, 9*(2), 102–112.

Scruggs, T. E., & Mastropieri, M. A. (1996). Teacher perceptions of mainstreaming/inclusion, 1958–1995. *Exceptional Children, 63*, 59–74.

Shores, R. E., Gunter, P. L., & Jack, S. L. (1993). Classroom management strategies: Are they setting events for coercion. *Behavioral Disorders, 18*(2), 92–102.

Skiba, R. J., Peterson, R. L., & Williams, T. (1997). Office referrals and suspension: Disciplinary intervention in middle schools. *Education and Treatment of Children, 20*, 295–315.

Spaulding, S. A., Horner, R. H., Irvin L. K., May, S. L., Emeldi, M., Tobin, T. J., et al. (in press). Schoolwide social-behavioral climate, student problem behavior, support needs, and related administrative decision-making: Empirical patterns from 2005–06 database on 1709 schools nationwide. *Journal of Positive Behavior Interventions.*

Sprague, J. R., & Golly, A. (2004). *Best Behavior: Building positive behavior support in schools.* Longmont, CO: Sopris West Educational Services.

Sprick, R., & Garrison, M. (2008). *Interventions: Evidence-based behavioral strategies for individual students* (2nd ed.). Eugene, OR: Pacific Northwest.

Sprick, R., Garrison, M., & Howard, L. (1998). *CHAMPs: A proactive and positive approach to classroom management.* Longmont, CO: Sopris West.

Stiggins, R., Arter, J. A., Chappius, J., & Chappius, S. (2007). *Classroom assessment for student learning: Doing it right—using it well.* Portland, OR: Educational Testing Service.

Sugai, G., & Horner, R. H. (2005). Schoolwide positive behavior supports: Achieving and sustaining effective learning environments for all students. In W. H. Heward (Ed.), *Focus on behavior analysis in education: Achievements, challenges, and opportunities* (pp. 90–102). Upper Saddle River, NJ: Pearson Prentice-Hall.

Teachman, B. A., & Smith-Janik, S. (2005). Extinction and habituation. In M. Hersen & J. Rosqvist (Eds.), *Encyclopedia of behavior modification and cognitive behavior therapy, Vol. 1* (pp. 292–296). Thousand Oaks, CA: Sage.

Watson, T. S., & Butler, T. S. (2005). Chaining. In M. Hersen, G. Sugai, & R. Horner (Eds.), *Encyclopedia of behavior modification and cognitive behavior therapy, Vol. 3* (pp. 1213–1216). Thousand Oaks, CA: Sage.

Weinstein, C. S., & Mignano, A. J. (2003). *Elementary classroom management: Lessons from research and practice* (3rd ed.). Boston: McGraw Hill.

# *Index*

**CORWIN**

A SAGE Company

The Corwin logo—a raven striding across an open book—represents the union of courage and learning. Corwin is committed to improving education for all learners by publishing books and other professional development resources for those serving the field of PreK–12 education. By providing practical, hands-on materials, Corwin continues to carry out the promise of its motto: **"Helping Educators Do Their Work Better."**